STATISTICS IN THE ENVIRONMENTAL SCIENCES

A symposium
sponsored by ASTM
Committee D-19 on Water
Philadelphia, Pa., 7–8 October 1982

ASTM SPECIAL TECHNICAL PUBLICATION 845
Steven M. Gertz, Roy F. Weston, Inc.,
and M. D. London, Public Service Electric
and Gas Company, editors

ASTM Publication Code Number (PCN)
04-845000-16

 1916 Race Street, Philadelphia, Pa. 19103

Library of Congress Cataloging in Publication Data

Statistics in the environmental sciences.

(ASTM special technical publication; 845)
Includes bibliographies and index.
1. Ecology—Statistical methods—Congresses.
2. Environmental monitoring—Statistical methods—
Congresses.   3. Environmental protection—Statistical
methods—Congresses.   I. Gertz, Steven M.   II. London,
M. D.   III. American Society for Testing and Materials.
Committee D-19 on Water.   IV. Series.
QH541.15.S72S73 1984   574.5′072   83-73439
ISBN 0-8031-0206-2

NOTE

The Society is not responsible, as a body,
for the statements and opinions
advanced in this publication.

Printed in Baltimore, Md. (b)
November 1984

Foreword

The symposium on Statistics in the Environmental Sciences was held in Philadelphia, Pennsylvania, 7–8 October 1982. The symposium was sponsored by ASTM Committee D-19 on Water. Steven M. Gertz, Roy F. Weston, Inc., presided as symposium chairman. Steven M. Gertz and M. D. London, Public Service Electric and Gas Company, are editors of this publication.

Related
ASTM Publications

Aquatic Toxicology and Hazard Assessment: Sixth Symposium, STP 802 (1983). 04-802000-16

Aquatic Toxicology and Hazard Assessment (Fifth Conference), STP 766 (1982), 04-766000-16

Native Aquatic Bacteria: Enumeration, Activity, and Ecology, STP 695 (1979), 04-695000-16

Methods and Measurements of Periphyton Communities: A Review, STP 690 (1978), 04-690000-16

Biological Data in Water Pollution Assessment: Quantitative and Statistical Analyses, STP 652 (1978), 04-652000-16

A Note of Appreciation
to Reviewers

The quality of the papers that appear in this publication reflects not only the obvious efforts of the authors but also the unheralded, though essential, work of the reviewers. On behalf of ASTM we acknowledge with appreciation their dedication to high professional standards and their sacrifice of time and effort.

ASTM Committee on Publications

ASTM Editorial Staff

Contents

Introduction

Mathematical and statistical techniques are important tools for the scientist and engineer to use in describing a given environment, describing an existing impact, predicting an impact, or ascertaining an environmental trend. Historically, however, these techniques were not used frequently, and many environmental studies were more qualitative than quantitative. Yet, in recent years the need to develop and use more quantitative mathematical and statistical analyses has become apparent to many investigators. This need occurred for many reasons, such as: the desire to effectively and objectively communicate the results of an investigation; the desire to have a consistent measurable base upon which to establish environmental rules and regulations; the needs of industry to analyze and predict environmental impacts; the desire to monitor the environment such that that program cost is minimized and information content is maximized; and so on. In an effort to respond to these needs, ASTM Subcommittee D19.01 on Statistical Methods organized a symposium entitled "Statistics In the Environmental Sciences."

This symposium was held in Philadelphia, Pennsylvania on 7–8 October 1982, and was divided into two parts. Part 1 was at ASTM Headquarters on 7 October 1982 and consisted of the invited papers. The topics covered there and reported on in this symposium volume include:

1. Statistical Ecology
2. Environmental Monitoring
3. Ecological Impact Assessment
4. Risk Assessment
5. Environmental Health
6. Quality Assurance
7. Computer Software

Part 2 of the symposium was held on 8 October 1982 at the offices of Roy F. Weston, Inc., in West Chester, Pennsylvania. This segment began with a panel discussion on "A Proposed Cooperative Program on Statistical Ecology and Environmental Statistics" which is presented in this volume. The panel discussion was then followed by a series of workshops which examined in detail the topics presented in Part 1.

The purpose of this symposium and this publication is to provide a forum for scientists engaged in and scientists interested in learning more about the development and application of mathematical and statistical techniques to environmental problems. Emphasis was placed on the conceptual framework of applying statistical analyses but not at the expense of mathematical rigor. Rather, the approach taken emphasized the types of analyses available, their usefulness under a variety of conditions, and the decision making process an investigator must go through prior to applying the techniques.

The papers presented in this volume will hopefully be useful to those engaged in a variety of environmental studies. Overall, this volume should be particularly useful to the biologist, toxicologist, and environmental engineer since it provides guidance in the design of environmental studies programs and the evaluation and interpretation of subsequent data. It should also prove useful to regulatory personnel, industrial scientists and engineers, and professor and student alike.

Steven M. Gertz

Roy F. Weston, Inc., West Chester, Pa. 19380.

G. P. Patil[1]

Some Perspectives of Statistical Ecology and Environmental Statistics*

REFERENCE: Patil, G. P., **"Some Perspectives of Statistical Ecology and Environmental Statistics,"** *Statistics in the Environmental Sciences, ASTM STP 845,* S. M. Gertz and M. D. London, Eds., American Society for Testing and Materials, 1984, pp. 3–22.

ABSTRACT: The paper sets the scene with historical and professional organizational perspectives briefly describing the activities and publications of groups concerned with statistical ecology and environmental statistics. Then follow the scientific perspectives with examples illustrating certain basic issues and features arising in ecological and environmental work. The observational studies, visibility bias, and inferential recovery constitute a critical problem area. It is discussed at some length with examples and data sets. Extrapolation issues constitute another critical problem area. Different kinds of extrapolation are briefly discussed with examples of low-dose extrapolation and calculated virtually safe dose levels. An example of recruitment distributions and inferences about long-term yields is also given. The issue of single versus several models is touched upon. The present day status of the subject of quantitative risk analysis is briefly described. A need for a focal cooperative program in statistical ecology and environmental statistics is identified.

KEY WORDS: statistical ecology, environmental statistics, cooperative program, size-biased sampling, weighted distributions, observational bias, extrapolation issues, risk analysis, recruitment distributions, virtual safe dose levels

The third quarter of the twentieth century proceeded with a sense of achievement in matters of productivity and prosperity and dreamed of leisure and enriched life in the near future. The fourth quarter of the twentieth century has seen only nightmares so far! Within this complex mosaic of science, technol-

*Based on the keynote speech given at the inaugural of the ASTM Symposium on Statistics and the Environmental Sciences. This paper was prepared while the author was under partial support from the National Marine Fisheries Service on a project entitled, Stochastics and Statistics in Marine Fisheries Research and Management, under contract NA-80-FAC-00040.

[1]Professor of Mathematical Statistics, Department of Statistics and the Graduate Program in Ecology, The Pennsylvania State University, University Park, Pa. 16802.

ogy, and the society, we need to be pursuing statistics, ecology, and the environment with a firm and full view of productivity, prosperity, and quality. I would like to share with you some of my perspectives of statistical ecology and environmental statistics—a subject area that has acquired importance in view of the current ecological and environmental issues.

The subject area of statistical ecology and environmental statistics is relatively young. Various interdisciplinary efforts and activities by concerned professional organizations have been instrumental in the promotion of scientific dialogues and in the dissemination of the results in an impressive variety of valuable publications. Among others, the following organizations and groups come to mind in this connection: the Committee on Statistics and the Environment of the American Statistical Association, the SIAM Institute for Mathematics and Society, the Mathematical Ecology Group in Great Britain, and the International Statistical Ecology Program of the International Association for Ecology, the International Statistical Institute, and the International Biometric Society. Broadly speaking, the latter two groups have so far emphasized statistical ecology in their programs, whereas the former have had primary emphasis on environmental statistics.

Publications listed at the end of this paper can give an idea of these timely and useful volumes [1-24]. They bring home the underlying unity in diversity while effectively making available in one place the enormous material of an interdisciplinary nature. This is what most everyone would like to know. Having these volumes around is extremely worthwhile.

Most everyone would like to know of the proposed cooperative program on statistical ecology and environmental statistics for increased resource productivity and environmental protection. The present symposium has a full scale panel discussion on the proposed program, and a special paper prepared for the purposes of this volume. It would give an idea of what could be done together to meet the challenge of statistics, ecology, and the environment.

Certain Scientific Perspectives Through Examples

While effort within a single discipline is not necessarily easy, interdisciplinary research and training tend to be even more difficult. The following stories may help convey some of the flavor and essence of an interdisciplinary effort.

Comprehensive Versus Comprehensible

Consider the following. We wish to comprehend a given situation.

1. For lack of information, we do not (quite) comprehend the situation.

2. We collect information, and we tend to collect comprehensive information.

3. Because the information is comprehensive, we do not (quite) comprehend it.

4. So we summarize the information through a set of indices (statistics) so that it would be comprehensible.

5. But now, we do not comprehend quite what the indices exactly mean.

6. And, therefore, we do not (quite) comprehend the situation.

7. Thus, without (all) information, or with (partial) information, or with summarized information, we do not quite comprehend a situation!

This dilemma is not to suggest a bleak picture for one's ability to understand, predict, or manage a situation in the face of uncertainty. It is more to suggest a need to state clearly the purpose, formulation, and solution for the study under consideration.

Information Paradox

Generally speaking, we have infinite information around us; but often we do not quite know what to make of it. At the same time, however, for a specific problem, we may have an infinitesimal amount of information. Often, we do not quite know what to make of it either. We find ourselves in need of additional information, even when we know of the infinite information around us.

Is there a satisfactory resolution of the paradox?

How Many of Them Are Out There?

This scenario takes place in a court of law. The issue is about the abundance of species seemingly endangered, threatened, or rare. The judge orders an investigation. A seasoned investigator conducts the survey. He reports having seen 375 individual members of the species under consideration. The judge invites comments.

Industrial Lobby—The reported record of 375 members makes sense. The visibility factor is low in such surveys. The investigator has surely missed most of them that are out there. The exploitation should not cause alarm.

Environmental Lobby—The reported record of 375 makes sense. The investigator is an expert in such surveys. He has observed and recorded most of them that are there. And, therefore, only a few are out there. The species population needs to be protected.

The scenario is a typical one. It brings home the issues characteristic of field observations often lacking a sampling frame necessary for the classical sampling theory to apply. One needs to work with visibility analysis instead. Satisfactory estimation of biological population abundance depends, in such cases, largely on adequate measurement of visibility, variously termed catchability, audibility, etc. And, this is not a trivial problem!

Where Do They Go?

Someone, concerned about the typical direction in which disoriented birds of a certain species fly, goes out in an open field, stands facing north, and observes a bird vanish at the horizon at an angle of 10 deg. A little later he finds a second bird vanish at the horizon at an angle of 350 deg. He obtains the average $(10 + 350)/2 = 180$ deg and declares that south is the typical direction. Figure 1, however, reveals that this analysis is wrong. North is in fact a typical direction based on the evidence. What is wrong? And where?... This extremely simple example has an astonishingly deep message in it: make sure that the modeling and analysis protocol do not mismatch or contradict the basics of the protocol of the phenomenon that is being modeled.

Martian Philosophy

A student wishes to study "Martian philosophy" but finds that there is no instructional program available in Martian philosophy. He is advised to take courses in astronomy, which may have some bearing upon Mars; he is also asked to take courses in philosophy that may have some context of the universe; and in due course, he is declared to have completed a program in Martian philosophy! The inadequacy of this approach is clear. It would be important to make sure that neither the student nor the supervisor falls into this trap. Integrated and interactive research training programs should be made available to those interested and concerned.

Observational Studies, Visibility Bias, and Inferential Recovery with Examples

Ecological surveys and environmental studies, unlike most of the socioeconomic survey work, frequently lack a sampling frame for the populations under study. Observational mechanisms become procedures of unequal probability sampling without a sampling frame for reasons of differential visibility, audibility, or catchability. The original distribution produced by nature, thus, may not be reproduced when an investigator collects a sample of observations.

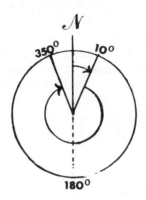

FIG. 1—*North is a typical direction.*

The main interest in any investigation is, however, to determine the characteristics of the original distribution. Further, it also becomes important to assess the distortion caused in determining these characteristics in case the change in the underlying distribution due to sampling bias is ignored. Some of these issues and examples are briefly discussed. A demonstration project on sex ratio is given along with the analysis of the data collected at the Symposium. The observational studies aspect in statistical ecology and environmental statistics is a critical problem area needing careful attention and effort.

Size-Biased Sampling and Weighted Distributions

Size-biased sampling arises in ecological and environmental work quite often. A common feature in the discrete case is that individuals are sampled, whereas aggregate observations are recorded on groups to which the individuals belong, such as, herds, families, species, etc. In the continuous case, a common feature is that the sampling unit for which a measurement is recorded is not selected at random from the population of units, but through a built-in mechanism that makes the selection probability proportional to the recorded measurement of the unit.

Suppose X is a nonnegative observable random variable (rv) with its natural probability density function $f(x; \theta)$, where θ is the natural parameter. Suppose a realization x of X under $f(x; \theta)$ enters the investigator's record with probability proportional to $w(x, \beta)$, so that

$$\text{prob(recording} | X = y) \div \text{prob(recording} | X = x) \\ = w(y, \beta) \div w(x, \beta)$$

Here the recording (weight) function $w(x, \beta)$ is a nonnegative function with parameter β representing the recording (sighting) mechanism. Clearly, the recorded x is not an observation on X, but on the rv X^w, say, having pdf

$$f^w(x; \theta, \beta) = \frac{w(x, \beta)f(x; \theta)}{\omega}$$

where ω is the normalizing factor. The rv X^w is called the weighted version of X, and its distribution is called the weighted distribution with weight function w. When $w(x, \beta) = x$, the weighted distribution is called the size-biased distribution with pdf

$$f^*(x; \theta) = \frac{xf(x; \theta)}{\mu}, \quad \mu = E[X]$$

and the corresponding sighting mechanism is called size-biased sampling. For further discussion and references, see Patil and Rao [25, 26].

Aerial Survey and Visibility Bias

The visibility bias is a recognized problem in aerial survey techniques for estimating wildlife population density and for studying animal behavior. The visibility bias is present because of the failure to observe some animals. A sampling model requires: (*a*) animals occur in groups of varying sizes, (*b*) each animal has probability β of being observed, and (*c*) conditional on observing at least one member of a group, the entire group is observed with certainty. A parameter of interest may be the mean group size. If the group size X has *pdf* $f(x; \theta)$, then, under the above assumptions, the distribution of the recorded group size X^w has *pdf* $f^w(x; \theta, \beta)$ with weight function $w(x, \beta) = 1 - (1 - \beta)^x$. As $\beta \rightarrow 0$, the limit of $f^w(x; \theta, \beta)$ assumes the size-biased form $f^*(x; \theta)$.

For further discussion of the problems and available solutions, see Cook and Martin [27] and Patil and Rao [25,26].

Resource Utilization Surveys

In assessing the extent of utilization of the national parks, tourist hotels, and other recreational facilities, an investigator asks a tourist how long he has been visiting the location. The data so recorded on a sample of tourists have the size-biased feature. This is because tourists with longer duration visits come into the record with larger probabilities than those with shorter duration visits. It is considered reasonable to assume the encounter probability to be proportional to the duration.

One could avoid introducing such a size-bias by asking the question to each departing individual instead, at the exit. But, then, this would require the investigator to invest considerable survey time.

For further discussion of the problems and available solutions, see Mahfoud, Patil, and Ratnaparkhi [28], Morrison [29], and Patil and Rao [25].

In 1966, a survey research agency undertook a statistical survey on tourism in a certain country. One of the main objectives of this investigation was to estimate the mean sojourn time per tourist. Due to the lack of a sampling frame and the high mobility of the tourists, it was decided to sample them where they could be easily reached. So two types of surveys were conducted simultaneously. In one survey, the tourists were sampled in the hotels where they were residing, and in the other survey, the sample was selected at different frontier stations from tourists who were about to end their journey in the country. In both cases, it was assumed that the selection procedure adopted would produce random samples. It turned out, however, that the observed mean sojourn time ($\mu = 17.8$ days per tourist) obtained from the survey in the hotels was practically twice the observed mean sojourn time ($\mu = 9.0$ days per tourist) computed from the sample obtained at the frontier stations.

No explanation was given as to what might have caused these two estimates to differ so much. Both estimates were based on large sample sizes: 12 321 tourists from the frontier stations and 3 000 from the hotels. Suspected by the officials in the Department of Planning, the estimate from the hotels was discarded.

It was overlooked then that the sampling scheme in the hotels did not lead to a random sample of observations on the sojourn time because it gave larger probability of selection to those tourists with longer residence time in the hotels. If this phenomenon were realized, an adequate estimator of the mean sojourn time would have been developed, thus preventing the sacrifice of 20% of the total collected information.

Trait of Interest and Family Size

If we wish to study the distribution of albino children in families capable of producing such children, we may contact a large number of families and ascertain from each family the number of albinos. But, this method of investigation is wasteful. A convenient method in such a case is first to discover an albino child and through it obtain the information about the family to which the child belongs. But such a procedure may not give equal chance to all families in which albinos have occurred. The exact chance for a family with x albinos is that of detecting at least one of its albino children, which may be equal to $w(x, \beta) = 1 - (1 - \beta)^x$, where β is the probability of an encounter with an albino child. As $\beta \rightarrow 0$, the limit of $f^w(x: \theta, \beta)$ assumes the size-biased form $f^*(x; \theta)$.

For further discussion of the problems and available solutions, see Patil and Rao [26] and Stene [30].

Family Size and Sex Ratio

Various demographic and social studies involve family size and sex ratio as important factors which have some bearing on main study. Let us ascertain from each male student in a class the number of brothers, including himself, and the sisters he has. Denote by k the number of reporting male students, and by B and S the total number of brothers and sisters reported. The characteristics of the population of interest are: (a) the male sex ratio, and (b) the mean family size (number of children).

The data in Table 1 are from Patil and Rao [26]. For each city indicated, it gives the number k of male respondents with the number of brothers B and the number of sisters S reported.

Under the usual binomial model, $B/(B + S)$ would give the unbiased estimate of the male sex ratio, whereas, $(B + S)/k$ would estimate the mean family size. However, under size-biased sampling, these become over-estimates. Corrected estimates for the sex ratio are $(B - k)/(B + S - k)$, whereas the corrected estimates for the mean family size are given by the harmonic means (δ) of the reported family sizes for each city.

We note that the values of $(B + k)/(B + S - k)$ are closer to 1/2, and that

TABLE 1—*Estimates of sex ratio and family size from data on male respondents.*

Place and Year		k	B	S	$\dfrac{B}{B+S}$	$\dfrac{B-k}{B+S-k}$	$\dfrac{B+S}{k}$	δ
Delhi	:75	29	92	66	0.58	0.488	5.45	4.25
Calcutta	:63	104	414	312	0.57	0.498	6.96	5.30
Waltair	:69	39	123	88	0.58	0.488	5.41	4.36
Hyderabad	:74	25	72	53	0.58	0.470	5.00	3.46
Tirupati (students)	:75	592	1902	1274	0.60	0.507	5.36	4.24
Tirupati (staff)	:76	50	172	130	0.57	0.484	6.04	4.20
Poona	:75	47	125	65	0.66	0.545	4.04	3.15
Tehran	:75	21	65	40	0.62	0.500	5.00	3.18
Isphahan	:75	11	45	32	0.58	0.515	7.00	5.70
Tokyo	:75	50	90	34	0.73	0.540	2.48	2.25
Columbus	:75	29	65	52	0.62	0.523	4.00	2.79
State College	:75	28	80	37	0.68	0.584	4.18	3.21
College Station	:76	63	152	90	0.63	0.497	3.84	3.04
London and Bradford	:76	43	80	39	0.67	0.487	2.77	2.15

NOTE—It has not been possible to ascertain the actual family sizes in the populations of different cities quoted in the Table except in the cases of Indian cities. In these cases the figures were close to δ, as predicted.

the δ estimates are consistently smaller than the $(B + S)/k$ estimates as expected. For further discussion, see Rao [31] and Patil and Rao [26].

A Demonstration Project at the ASTM Symposium

The symposium participants were asked to report on the number of brothers and sisters they have, and also on the number of sons and daughters they have. The data in Table 2 and the resulting calculations speak for themselves!

From This to That, But Precisely to What? Extrapolation and Related Issues with Examples

Like in most every other field, problems in statistical ecology and environmental statistics prominently involve extrapolation issues and the related exploratory effort on "from what you know/observe to what you need/wish to know and can determine/decide." Broadly speaking, general extrapolation amounts to a transfer of some property/attribute from one setup to another, and in so doing, the issues of validity, sensitivity, and robustness arise.

If we should wish to consider different categories of extrapolation, we might choose to speak of system extrapolation, model extrapolation, and inference extrapolation. The following summary description may be of interest here. It would be also of interest to examine the examples of earlier sections and attempt the implicit extrapolation categorization.

TABLE 2—*Report on numbers of brothers and sisters.*

		Males Reporting					
(A)	Brothers	Sisters	B	S	B	S	B	S
	2	1	2	0	5	1	1	0
	2	2	4	0	1	0	2	1
	5	3	1	1	1	4	4	5
	3	2	1	0	1	2	2	0
	1	0	1	1	2	1	1	1

$$B = 42, \quad S = 25, \quad k = 20$$

$$\text{Reported male ratio} = \frac{42}{67} \approx \frac{2}{3}; \qquad \text{Corrected male ratio} = \frac{42-20}{67-20} = \frac{22}{47} \approx \frac{1}{2}$$

(B)	Sons	Daughters	S	D	S	D	S	D
	0	0	1	1	1	1	0	0
	1	0	3	3	0	2	1	0
	0	1	0	1	2	0	0	0
	0	0	0	0	2	2	1	1
	1	1	1	1	0	0	1	1

$$S = 15, \quad D = 15, \quad k = 20$$

$$\text{Estimated male ratio} = \frac{15}{30} = \frac{1}{2}$$

	Females Reporting	
(A) Brothers:	0 0 1 1 3	$B = 5, \quad S = 12, \quad k = 5.$
		$\text{Corrected female ratio} = \dfrac{12-5}{17-5} = \dfrac{7}{12} \approx \dfrac{1}{2}$
Sisters:	1 1 4 1 5	

(B) Sons:	4 0 0 0 1	$S = 5, \quad D = 1$
Daughters:	0 0 0 0 1	
		$\text{Estimated female ratio} = \dfrac{1}{6}$

System Extrapolation

Extrapolation from one system/setup to another may be identified to be the system extrapolation, with examples, such as: mouse to man, microcosm to nature, laboratory to nature, computer to nature, map to nature, paper-pencil to nature, etc. The common denominator essentially turns out to be the extrapolation from study-generated data to estimates of human or ecological risks.

Model Extrapolation

Extrapolation from one model to another or alternately from one region to another may be identified to be the model extrapolation, with examples, such as: low-dose response extrapolation, time series extrapolation, how much resource extrapolation (oil, fish, . . .), etc.

Inference Extrapolation

Extrapolation involving different possible samples or different possible inferential methods may be identified to be the inference extrapolation. The secular parable of the elephant and the blind men provides a vivid example. It brings out with great eloquence and clarity the dilemmas and the difficulties surrounding the dialogue and the debate around the issues involving sampling, modeling, and analysis whether in theory, practice, or in the interaction of the two. It is a story to recall and to ponder whenever one is engaged in any extrapolation in the face of uncertainty, and in its communication.

The Blind Men and the Elephant
by J. G. Saxe (1816–1887)

It was six men of Indostan
To learning much inclined,
Who went to see the Elephant
(Though all of them were blind),
That each by observation
Might satisfy his mind.

The First approached the Elephant,
And happening to fall
Against his broad and sturdy side,
At once began to bawl:
"God bless! but the Elephant
Is very like a wall!"

The Second, feeling of the tusk,
Cried, "Ho! what have we here
So very round and smooth and sharp?
To me 'tis mighty clear
This wonder of an Elephant
Is very like a spear!"

The Third approached the animal,
And happening to take
The squirming trunk within his hands,
Thus boldly up and spake:
"I see," quoth he, "the Elephant
Is very like a Snake!"

The Fourth reached out an eager hand,
And felt about the knee.
"What most this wondrous beast is like
Is mighty plain," quoth he;
"'Tis clear enough the Elephant
Is very like a tree!"

The Fifth who chanced to touch the ear,
Said: "E'en the blindest man
Can tell what this resembles most;
Deny the fact who can,
This marvel of an Elephant
Is very like a fan!"

The Sixth no sooner had begun
About the beast to grope,
Than, seizing on the swinging tail
That fell within his scope,
"I see," quoth he, "the Elephant
Is very like a rope!"

And so these men of Indostan
Disputed loud and long,
Each in his own opinion
Exceeding stiff and strong.
Though each was partly in the right
And all were in the wrong!

Low Dose Extrapolation Problem

Substantive effort has gone into the subject area of estimating low-dose effects and in the building of the needed dose-response models. The low dose extrapolation problem arises when extrapolation is made from the observed high dose-response region to the unobserved/unobservable low dose-response region. Several plausible models are fitted to the observed high dose-response data, and corresponding virtual safe dose (VSD) levels are estimated at stipulated low response/risk levels. Response is usually measured by the probability of the animal showing toxic response to the applied dose level. Four dose-response models have been used for a typical animal chronic bioassay. They are: one-hit model, multistage model, multihit model, and Weibull model. It should be of interest to examine the performance of these models. The tabulated summaries in Table 3 are based on Van Ryzin [32]. It is worthwhile to give them a closer look. For further details, see Van Ryzin.

Van Ryzin has commented that in every case the smallest estimate of VSD was given by the one-hit model, the second smallest by the multistage, the second largest by the Weibull, and the largest by the multihit. This ordering is not unique with these three data sets. Finally, he summarizes by saying: "The use

TABLE 3—*Summary of dose-response models.*

(A) Results for Dimethylnitrosamine

	Estimates of VSD in ppm at Risk Level		
Model	10^{-4}	10^{-6}	10^{-8}
One-hit	3.1×10^{-3}	3.1×10^{-5}	3.1×10^{-7}
Multistage	5.7×10^{-3}	5.7×10^{-5}	5.7×10^{-7}
Multihit	1.3×10^{-1}	1.2×10^{-2}	1.0×10^{-3}
Weibull	4.6×10^{-2}	1.8×10^{-3}	7.3×10^{-5}

(B) Results for DDT

	Estimates of VSD in ppm at Risk Level		
Model	10^{-4}	10^{-6}	10^{-8}
One-hit	2.7×10^{-2}	2.7×10^{-4}	2.7×10^{-6}
Multistage	6.4×10^{-2}	6.4×10^{-4}	6.4×10^{-6}
Multihit	7.6×10^{-1}	4.9×10^{-2}	3.2×10^{-3}
Weibull	4.4×10^{-1}	1.8×10^{-2}	7.6×10^{-4}

(C) Results for Ethylene Thiourea

	Estimates of VSD in ppm at Risk Level		
Model	10^{-4}	10^{-6}	10^{-8}
One-hit	5.4×10^{-2}	5.4×10^{-4}	5.4×10^{-6}
Multistage	20.8	4.5	1.2
Multihit	60.0	33.5	18.4
Weibull	25.0	6.3	1.6

of a variety of models to get answers in or near the experimental range is advocated, followed by linear extrapolation based on other judgements." The purpose of this paper was merely to review some of the available recently developed models for low-dose extrapolation and to show how they behave when applied to data.

In his recent paper on statistical issues in toxicology, Hoel [33] provides a lucid description of the state-of-the-art of the subject area and comments: "Possibly the most interesting and certainly the most controversial statistical activity in toxicology has occurred in the area of risk extrapolation in the past few years.... Considerable faith is required to accept the extrapolated estimates, since the mathematical models needed for this type of activity are crude approximations at best and misleading in many cases. The most pressing need is for reasonable measures of precision which incorporate both the statistical errors in the data and more importantly, the biological model errors." The following tabulation (Table 4) from Hoel compares point estimates for two of the more popular mechanistic models using some of the best available rodent

TABLE 4—*Estimated virtually safe dose at 10^{-6}.*

Substance	Gamma Multihit	Multistage	Ratio VSD for Multihit/Multistage
NTA	8.0×10^{-1}	1.9×10^{-4}	4.2×10^{3}
Aflatoxin B$_1$	2.8×10^{-1}	7.9×10^{-4}	3.5×10^{2}
DMN	7.7×10^{-2}	1.9×10^{-3}	4.0×10^{1}
Vinyl chloride	3.9×10^{-10}	2.0×10^{-2}	2.0×10^{-8}
BCME	3.7×10^{-2}	4.0×10^{-4}	9.3×10^{1}
Saccharin	1.1	3.3×10^{-1}	3.3
Ethylenethiourea	$3.3 \times 10^{+1}$	4.5	7.3
Dieldrin	6.3×10^{-3}	2.2×10^{-5}	2.9×10^{2}
DDT	4.8×10^{-2}	6.4×10^{-4}	7.5×10^{1}

data. He observes from the table that considerable discrepancies are common, with some being several orders of magnitude in size.

The papers by Chand and Hoel [34], Crump [35], Land [36], Neyman [37], Rai and Van Ryzin [38] would be of further interest in matters of model building, model comparison and extrapolation for determining safe levels of environmental agents.

Recruitment Distributions and Inferences About Long-Term Yields

Various situations arise in statistical ecology that involve different kinds of extrapolation. Consider, for example, the problem of recruitment distributions and inferences about long-term yields in marine fisheries. I would like to briefly share with you some of the highlights of my current research with Charles Taillie in cooperation with Bradford Brown and Richard Hennemuth of the Northeast Fisheries Center at Woods Hole.

Hennemuth, Palmer, and Brown [39] reviewed recruitment data for eighteen fish stocks around the world by examining the observed frequency distributions. Taillie and Patil [40] continued the statistical analysis. The data are examined from several vantage points, such as, skewness, kurtosis, and bimodality. Motivated by a variety of ecological and statistical considerations, ten families of distributions have been fitted to the eighteen recruitment data sets. It is rather encouraging that all of them appear to be satisfactory in general. The ten models are: (*a*) lognormal (LN), (*b*) gamma (GAM), (*c*) type N catastrophe model (N), (*d*) mixture of two homoscedastic normals (MIX), (*e*) beta type two with a scale parameter (BETA), (*f*) symmetric-in-index parameters beta type two with a scale parameter (SBETA), (*g*) reciprocal gamma (RGAM), (*h*) weighted gamma type one (RG1), (*i*) weighted gamma type two (RG), and (*j*) weighted gamma type three (ATAN).

The purpose of this study has been to investigate long-term recruitment for its potential use in long-term planning of fisheries development and management. The specific purpose is twofold: (*a*) to be able to identify the long-run frequency distributions of recruitment without regard to time, and (b) to gain long-range insights that such a simplifying assumption should have to offer. Patil and Taillie [41] have adopted the following approach for making inferences about long-term yields.

Let the recruitment X have the equilibrium pdf $f(x) - f_X(x)$. We define $\bar{F}(c) = \text{prob}(X > c)$ to be the tail area of the pdf f to the right of c. Further, we define the tail distribution of the pdf f to the right of c to be the conditional distribution of X given that X exceeds c.

Let $x_1, x_2, \ldots, x_n$ be the random sample assumed to have come from the recruitment equilibrium pdf $f(x)$ over the n-year period 1, 2, $\ldots$, n. Let $x_{(1,n)} \leq x_{(2,n)} \leq \ldots \leq x_{(n,n)}$ be the ordered sample of the observed recruitment values. For the purposes of predicting good year, good year frequency, and good year size, one needs to define what one means by "good year," "good year frequency," and "good year size." We give here one of the definitions adopted, and resulting analysis in brief.

The good year of order j is defined to be the year with recruitment greater than $x_{(j,n)}$. The good year frequency of order j is defined by the tail area of f to the right of $x_{(j,n)}$. The good year size of order j is defined by the median of the tail distribution of f to the right of $x_{(j,n)}$. We conceptualize the large, medium, or low versions of good year size by the good year sizes of order n, $n - 1$, and $n - 2$, respectively. Thus, for each fish stock, a definition of good year corresponding to a plausible model provides a corresponding good year frequency and a good year size. We should assess the performance of these ten good-fitting models on the basis of their predictive capabilities of the good years, and their frequencies and sizes. Four specific questions that we wish to raise and seek answers for are the following:

1. Is there a trade off between the predictions of good year frequency and good year size as predicted by a model for a fish stock?
2. How do the models compare among themselves on their prediction of good year frequencies?
3. How do the models compare among themselves on their prediction of good year sizes?
4. To what extent are the comparisons based on the good year frequencies and sizes due to the mathematical tail behaviors of the models used?

While the work is in progress, Table 5 might provide some idea regarding predicted good year sizes and related issues of extrapolation, such as validity, sensitivity, robustness, etc.

Quantitative Risk Analysis

The language and framework of risk analysis have come into more and more use in the recent past, and it appears that the risk analysis approach is here to stay. The analysis of risks is being viewed increasingly as a field in itself, and

TABLE 5—*Good year size predictions for certain fish stocks (based on largest order statistic).*

Model Stock	RG	TN	MIX	ATAN	RG1	BETA	LN	SBETA	GAM	RGAM	Best Fit
1	3.76	3.76	3.78	3.87	3.96	3.96	4.03	4.03	3.96	4.11	MIX
2	4.17	4.17	4.20	4.17	4.16	4.91	4.56	4.60	4.33	4.91	RG
3	8.96	8.99	9.07	8.83	9.66	11.52	9.59	9.94	8.66	11.52	RG
4	3.59	3.54	3.64	3.53	3.97	4.39	3.93	4.00	3.66	4.39	RG
5	50.1	50.8	58.2	50.3	52.0	52.0	77.4	81.9	52.0	384	TN

the demand for a more orderly and formal treatment of risks is great. The Society for Risk Analysis is now in its fourth year, and its journal, *Risk Analysis*, provides a focal point for new developments in risk analysis for scientists from a wide range of disciplines. The journal covers topics of great interest to regulators, researchers, and scientific administrators. It deals with health risks, engineering, mathematical and theoretical aspects of risks, and social and psychological aspects of risks such as risk perception, acceptability, economics, and ethics.

Ruckelshaus in his major policy speech to the National Academy of Sciences on the subject of science, risk, and public policy has brought the role and use of risk analysis approach into a perceptive focus. He says, "Somehow our democratic technological society must resolve the dissonance between science and the creation of public policy. Nowhere is this more troublesome than in the formal assessment of risk—the estimation of the association between the exposure to a substance and the incidence of some disease, based on scientific data.... In assessing a suspected carcinogen, for example, there are uncertainties at every point where an assumption must be made.... One thing we clearly need to do is insure that our laws reflect these scientific realities.... Given the necessity of acting in the face of enormous scientific uncertainties, it is more important than ever that our scientific analysis be rigorous and the quality of our data be high.... Lest anyone misunderstand, I am not suggesting that all the elements of managing risk can be reduced to some neat mathematical formula. Going through a disciplined approach can help. It will assist in organizing our thoughts to include all the elements that should be weighed. We will build up a set of precedents that will assist later decision-making and provide more predictable outcomes for any social regulatory programs we adopt ..."

Barnthouse et al [42] define, "ecological risk analysis as the process of identifying and quantifying probabilities of adverse ecological change resulting from human activities or natural catastrophies. By emphasizing probabilities and by explicitly quantifying uncertainties, risk analysis can provide a more rational basis for environmental assessment and regulation. Ecological risk analysis can be used to: (*a*) estimate probabilities of compliance with environmental standards, (*b*) set standards based on probabilities of exceeding effects thresholds, (c) optimize research programs related to ecological hazards, (d) aid in making decisions about facility designs and mitigating strategies, and (e) decide which laboratory/microcosm measures to attempt to track in the field."

O'Connor and Swanson [43] discuss unreasonable degradation of the marine environment in the context of the 1977 Marine Protection, Research, and Sanctuaries Act. They present a strategy to quantify the extent of pollutant degradation in coastal environments and ecosystems. They recommend twelve indices as efficient and geographically comparable ways to characterize pollutant degradation. The indices are also recommended as scales of degradation along which "serious" or "unreasonable" degradation, in a social or legal sense, can be defined by legislative, regulatory, and judicial processes.

Hennemuth [44] draws a picturesque analogy between health risks and ecological risks. He suggests, ". . . our need is to organize and define our activities to better define biological effects of pollution. This is complicated by the fact that we don't know what all the pollutants are; therefore, we are in a position analogous to a Doctor who has an unconscious patient wheeled into his examining room and is called on to diagnose what his problem is and to recommend an appropriate treatment. There is a need for selecting thinking processes, strategies, and statistical methods appropriate to such a situation . . ."

Brown and Patil [45] provide a broad overview of quantitative risk analysis in ecological research and management together with a pragmatic example from marine fisheries research and management.

Straf [2] provides a special issue of *American Statistician* discussing some of the contemporary issues of statistics and the environment with primary emphasis on health effects. A new three year old journal of the Society for Risk Analysis is a good source for varied literature. For policy-related literature on risk analysis and technological hazards, see Covello and Abernathy [46] which provides a bibliography of over one thousand entries that have appeared in the past decade.

Interested readers concerned about the scientific concepts, issues, methods, and examples involving probabilistic risk assessment, health risk assessment, environmental risk assessment, and ecological risk assessment may wish to consult current literature in the risk area, starting from the sources just cited.

Coping with Uncertainty in Research, Training, and Management in Statistical Ecology and Environmental Statistics

A characteristic of the environment is its natural variability in space and time. It becomes difficult to separate "signal" from "noise." If a 2% depletion of stratosphere ozone were suddenly to occur, it has been suggested that an additional ten years of observations would be required before the event could be confirmed with 90% confidence.

Study-generated data usually form the basis for the determination that there is some hazard. However, these data are open to questions of interpretation because of a "black box" being present somewhere. One can only model the implicit uncertainty of the black box in a way it appears plausible. It is clear that one cannot speak of the model, but a family of plausible models leading to implied conclusions that may be close enough or somewhat apart.

I am reminded of a story attributed to President Truman. Upon his assuming the office of the President of the United States, he called in a chief advisor to advise. The advisor, with great skill and detail, briefed the President. On the one hand, he said, this and this, but on the other hand, he said, that and that. And that is how it went for the full session. After the advisor left, the President is said to have remarked to his aide that what he needed was an advisor who was one-handed!

This story, while simple, has a lot in it. Even on the issue of single versus several models and solutions! Whether by a single individual or several would also be important. And particularly in the remaining part of the twentieth century of which one aspect is certain. And that is the uncertainty aspect of it. And not only that, but uncertainty has a variety of faces including a face of unknowns also. It appears vital that the science and the art of educated guessing and decision making in the face of uncertainty become an integral part of one's background and being, whether general or special. This would go a long way to help resolve the issues and activities involving statistical ecology and environmental statistics before the resolutions, if any, and the involved efforts society could no longer bear!

Let us hope that with the lessons of the "Sputnik age" behind, we in the agencies, industries, academia, and the concerned public would successfully find ways and means to experiment and implement genuine cooperative efforts toward more desirable statistics, ecology, and environment in the overall setting of science, technology, and society. A proposed co-operative program on statistical ecology and environmental statistics for increased resource productivity and environmental protection discussed at the end of this volume could be one such effort. Could we give it a try? Together, we could do something that is timely and satisfying.

References

[1] "Third Symposium—Statistics and the Environment," *Journal of the Washington Academy of Sciences*, Washington Academy of Sciences, Vol. 64, No. 2, 1974.
[2] "Proceedings of the Sixth Symposium on Statistics and the Environment," M. Straf, Ed., *American Statistician*, Vol. 36, No. 3, 1982.
[3] "Proceedings of the Seventh Symposium on Statistics and the Environment," W. Hunter, Ed., *American Statistician*, Vol. 37, No. 4, 1983.
[4] *Epidemiology*, D. Ludwig and K. L. Cooke, Eds., Society for Industrial and Applied Mathematics, Philadelphia, Pa., 1975.
[5] *Energy: Mathematics and Models*, F. S. Roberts, Ed., Society for Industrial and Applied Mathematics, Philadelphia, Pa., 1976.
[6] *Time Series and Ecological Processes*, H. H. Shugart, Ed., Society for Industrial and Applied Mathematics, Philadelphia, Pa., 1978.

[7] *Environmetrics 81: Selected Papers*, Selected Papers from a Conference held in Alexandria, Va., 8-10 April, Society for Industrial and Applied Mathematics, Philadelphia, Pa., 1981.

[8] *Environmental Health: Quantitative Methods*, A. S. Whittemore, Ed., Society for Industrial and Applied Mathematics, Philadelphia, Pa., 1977.

[9] *Energy and Health*, A. S. Whittemore and N. E. Breslow, Eds., Society for Industrial and Applied Mathematics, Philadelphia, Pa., 1979.

[10] *Mathematical Models in Ecology*, J. N. R. Jeffers, Ed., Blackwell Scientific Publications, Oxford, 1972.

[11] Skellam, J. G., "Some Philosophical Aspects of Mathematical Modeling in Empirical Science with Special Reference to Ecology," in *Mathematical Models in Ecology*, J. N. R. Jeffers, Ed., Blackwell Scientific Publications, Oxford, 1972, pp. 13-28.

[12] *Environmental Biomonitoring, Assessment, Prediction, and Management—Certain Case Studies and Related Quantitative Issues*, J. Cairns, Jr., G. P. Patil, and W. E. Waters, Eds., a publication of the ISEP Satellite Program in Statistical Ecology, International Co-operative Publishing House, Fairland, Md., 1979.

[13] *Quantitative Population Dynamics*, D. G. Chapman and V. F. Gallucci, Eds., a publication of the ISEP Satellite Program in Statistical Ecology, International Co-operative Publishing House, Fairland, Md., 1981.

[14] *Spatial and Temporal Analysis in Ecology*, R. M. Cormack and J. K. Ord, Eds., a publication of the ISEP Satellite Program in Statistical Ecology, International Co-operative Publishing House, Fairland, Md., 1979.

[15] *Sampling Biological Populations*, R. M. Cormack, G. P. Patil, and D. S. Robson, Eds., a publication of the ISEP Satellite Program in Statistical Ecology, International Co-operative Publishing House, Fairland, Md., 1979.

[16] *Ecological Diversity in Theory and Practice*, J. F. Grassle, G. P. Patil, W. K. Smith, and C. Taillie, Eds., a publication of the ISEP Satellite Program in Statistical Ecology, International Co-operative Publishing House, Fairland, Md., 1979.

[17] *Systems Analysis of Ecosystems*, G. S. Innis and R. V. O'Neill, Eds., a publication of the ISEP Satellite Program in Statistical Ecology, International Co-operative Publishing House, Fairland, Md., 1979.

[18] *Compartmental Analysis of Ecosystem Models*, J. H. Matis, B. C. Patten, and G. C. White, Eds., a publication of the ISEP Satellite Program in Statistical Ecology, International Co-operative Publishing House, Fairland, Md., 1979.

[19] *Statistical Distributions in Ecological Work*, J. K. Ord, G. P. Patil, and C. Taillie, Eds., a publication of the ISEP Satellite Program in Statistical Ecology, International Co-operative Publishing House, Fairland, Md., 1979.

[20] *Multivariate Methods in Ecological Work*, L. Orloci, C. R. Rao, and W. M. Stiteler, Eds., a publication of the ISEP Satellite Program in Statistical Ecology, International Co-operative Publishing House, Fairland, Md., 1979.

[21] *Contemporary Quantitative Ecology and Related Ecometrics*, G. P. Patil and M. L. Rosenzweig, Eds., a publication of the ISEP Satellite Program in Statistical Ecology, International Co-operative Publishing House, Fairland, Md., 1979.

[22] *Spatial Patterns and Statistical Distributions*, G. P. Patil, E. C. Pielou, and W. E. Waters, Eds., Pennsylvania State University Press, University Park, Pa., 1971.

[23] *Sampling and Modeling Biological Populations and Population Dynamics*, G. P. Patil, E. C. Pielou, and W. E. Waters, Eds., Pennsylvania State University Press, University Park, Pa., 1971.

[24] *Many Species Populations, Ecosystems, and Systems Analysis*, G. P. Patil, E. C. Pielou, and W. E. Waters, Eds., Pennsylvania State University Press, University Park, Pa., 1971.

[25] Patil, G. P. and Rao, C. R., "The Weighted Distributions: A Survey of Their Applications," in *Applications of Statistics*, P. R. Krishnaiah, Ed., North-Holland Publishing Company, Leyden, the Netherlands, 1977, pp. 383-405.

[26] Patil, G. P. and Rao, C. R., "Weighted Distributions and Size-Biased Sampling with Applications to Wildlife Populations and Human Families," *Biometrics*, Vol. 34, No. 2, 1978, pp. 179-189.

[27] Cook, R. D. and Martin, F. B., "A Model for Quadrat Sampling with "Visibility Bias,"" *Journal of the American Medical Association*, Vol. 69, 1974, pp. 345-349.

[28] Mahfoud, M., Patil, G. P., and Ratnaparkhi, M. V., "On Some Applications of Weighted

Distributions in Ecology and Related Fields—A Review," in *Glimpses of Ecology*, J. S. Singh and B. Gopal, Eds., International Scientific Publications, Jaipur, India, 1978, pp. 519-529.

[29] Morrison, D. G., "Some Results for Waiting Times with an Application to Survey Data," *The American Statistician*, Vol. 27, 1973, pp. 226-227.

[30] Stene, J., "Probability Distributions Arising from the Ascertainment and Analysis of Data on Human Families and Other Groups," in *Statistical Distributions in Scientific Work*, Vol. 6, C. Taillie, G. P. Patil, and B. Baldessari, Eds., Reidel Publishing Company, Dordrecht and Boston, 1981, pp. 233-264.

[31] Rao, C. R., "A Natural Example of a Weighted Binomial Distribution," *American Statistician*, Vol. 31, 1977, pp. 24-26.

[32] Van Ryzin, J., "Quantitative Risk Assessment," *Journal of Occupational Medicine*, Vol. 22, No. 5, 1980, pp. 321-326.

[33] Hoel, D. G., "Statistical Issues in Toxicology," in *Environmetrics 81: Selected Papers*, selected papers from a conference, Alexandria, Va., 8-10 April, SIMS, 1981, pp. 248-257.

[34] Chand, N. and Hoel, D. G., "A Comparison of Models for Determining Safe Levels of Environmental Agents," in *Reliability and Biometry*, Society for Industrial and Applied Mathematics, Philadelphia, Pa., 1974, pp. 681-700.

[35] Crump, K. S., "Dose Response Problems in Carcinogenesis," *Biometrics*, Vol. 35, 1979, pp. 157-167.

[36] Land, C. E., "Estimating Cancer Risks from Low Doses of Ionizing Radiation," *Science*, Vol. 209, 1980, pp. 1197-1203.

[37] Neyman, J., "A View of Biometry: An Interdisciplinary Domain Concerned with Chance Mechanisms Operating in Living Organisms; Illustration: Urethan Carcinogenesis," in *Reliability and Biometry*, Society for Industrial and Applied Mathematics, Philadelphia, Pa., 1974, pp. 183-201.

[38] Rai, K. and Van Ryzin, J., "A Generalized Multihit Dose-Response Model for Low-Dose Extrapolation," *Biometrics*, Vol. 37, 1981, pp. 341-352.

[39] Hennemuth, R. C., Palmer, J. E., and Brown, B. E., "A Statistical Description of Recruitment in Eighteen Selected Fish Stocks, *Journal of the Northwest Atlantic Fisheries Science*, Vol. 1, 1980, pp. 101-111.

[40] Taillie, C. and Patil, G. P., "Modeling and Analysis of Recruitment Distributions," in *Stochastic and Statistics in Marine Fisheries Research and Management*, Interim Report NA-80-FAC-00040, NEFC, NMFS, Woods Hole, Ma., 1982.

[41] Patil, G. P. and Taillie, C., "Diversity as a Concept and Its Measurement," *Journal of the American Statistical Association*, Vol. 77, No. 379, 1982, pp. 548-567.

[42] Barnthouse, L. W., Suter, G. W., II, and O'Neill, R. V., "Ecological Risk Analysis: Prospects and Problems," Environmental Sciences Division, Oak Ridge National Laboratory, Oak Ridge, Tenn., 1983.

[43] O'Connor, J. S. and Swanson, R. L., "Unreasonable Degradation of the Marine Environment—What is it?," *Oceans*, Sept. 1982, pp. 1125-1132.

[44] Hennemuth, R. C., "Opening Remarks to the Northeast Fisheries Center Workshop on Risk Analysis in Fisheries Research and Management," Sandy Hook, N. J., 1983.

[45] Brown, B. E. and Patil, G. P., "Quantitative Risk Analysis in Ecological Research and Management," an invited presentation at the Annual Meetings of the American Statistical Association, Toronto, 1983.

[46] Covello, V. and Abernathy, M., "Risk Analysis and Technological Hazards: A Policy-Related Bibliography," in *Technological Risk Assessment*, P. Ricci, L. Sagan, and C. Whipple, Eds., Sijthoff and Noordhoff International Publishers, Leyden, the Netherlands, 1983.

Bibliography

Barouch, E. and Kaufman, G. M., "Estimation of Undiscovered Oil and Gas," in *Mathematical Aspects of Production and Distribution of Energy*, Peter D. Lax, Ed., American Math Society, Providence, R.I., 1977, pp. 77-91.

Berg, G. C. and Maillie, H. D., *Measurement of Risks*, Plenum Press, New York, 1980.

Christensen, S. W. et al, "Science and the Law: Confluence and Conflict on the Hudson River," *Environmental Impact Assessment Review*, Vol. 2, No. 1, 1981, pp. 63-88.

Testing for Effects of Chemicals on Ecosystems, Committee to Review Methods for Ecotoxicology, National Academy Press, Washington, D.C., 1981.

Dennis, B. and Patil, G. P., "Species Abundance, Diversity, and Environmental Predictability," in *Ecological Diversity in Theory and Practice,* J. F. Grassle, G. P. Patil, W. Smith, and C. Taillie, Eds., International Co-operative Publishing House, Fairland, Md., 1979, pp. 93-114.

Dennis, B. and Patil, G. P., "The Gamma Distribution and Weighted Multimodal Gamma Distributions as Models of Population Abundance," *Mathematical Biosciences,* Vol. 68, 1984, pp. 187-212.

Eberhardt, L. L., "Transect Methods for Population Studies, *Journal of Wildlife Management,* Vol. 42, 1978, pp. 1-31.

Gates, C. E., "Line Transect and Related Issues," in *Sampling Biological Populations,* R. M. Cormack, G. P. Patil, and D. S. Robson, Eds., International Co-operative Publishing House, Fairland, Md., 1979, pp. 71-154.

Hennemuth, R. C. and Patil, G. P., "Implementing Statistical Ecology Initiatives to Cope with Global Resource Impacts—An Introduction to the Concept and a Workplan," *Proceedings,* Conference on Renewable Resource Inventories for Monitoring Changes and Trends, John Bell and Toby Atterbury, Eds., Oregon State University, Corvallis, Oreg., 1983, pp. 374-378.

Holling, C. S., "The Functional Response of Predators to Prey Density and Its Role in Mimicry and Population Regulation," *Memoirs Entonological Society of Canada,* Vol. 45, 1965, pp. 5-60.

Hunter, J. S., "Environmental Monitoring," a report to the EPA from the Study Group on Environmental Monitoring, National Academy of Sciences, Washington, D.C., 1977.

Lewis, T. R., *Stochastic Modeling of Ocean Fisheries Resource Management,* University of Washington Press, Seattle, Wash., 1983.

May, R. M., "Island Biogeography and the Design of Wildlife Preserves," *Nature,* London, Vol. 254, 1975, pp. 177-178.

May, R. M., "Patterns of Species Abundance and Diversity," in *Ecology and Evolution of Communities,* M. L. Cody and J. M. Diamond, Eds., Harvard University Press, Cambridge, Mass., 1975, pp. 81-120.

Patil, G. P., Satellite Program in Statistical Ecology, *International Statistical Review,* Vol. 47, 1979, pp. 223-228.

Patil, G. P. and Taillie, C., "A Study of Diversity Profiles and Orderings for a Bird Community in the Vicinity of Colstrip, Montana," in *Contemporary Quantitative Ecology and Related Ecometrics,* G. P. Patil and M. L. Rosenzweig, Eds., International Co-operative Publishing House, Fairland, Md., 1979, pp. 23-47.

Patil, G. P., "Some Perspectives in Statistical Ecology," in *Ecologia,* A. Moroni, O. Ravera, and A. Anelli, Eds., SITE, Parma, Italy, 1981, pp. 181-187.

Patil, G. P., "Studies in Statistical Ecology Involving Weighted Distributions," *Proceedings of ISI Golden Jubilee,* Calcutta, India (to appear), 1983.

Patil, G. P., "International Statistical Ecology Program," in *Encyclopedia of Statistical Sciences,* S. Kotz and N. L. Johnson, Eds., Wiley, New York, 1984.

Patil, G. P. and Toombs, W., "General Education in the Face of Uncertainty, *Journal of General Education,* Vol. 34, 1982, pp. 234-246.

Simon, Richard, "Length Biased Sampling in Etiologic Studies," *American Journal of Epidemiology,* Vol. 111, No. 4, 1980, pp. 444-452.

Thomas, J. M., Mahaffey, J. A., Gore, K. L., and Watson, D. G., "Statistical Methods Used to Assess Biological Impact at Nuclear Power Plants," *Journal of Environmental Management,* Vol. 7, 1978, pp. 269-290.

Thomas, J. M., McKenzie, D. H., and Eberhardt, L. L., "Some Limitations of Biological Monitoring, *Environment International,* Vol. 5, 1981, pp. 3-10.

Warren, W. G., "Statistical Distributions in Forestry and Forest Products Research," in *Statistical Distributions in Scientific Work,* G. P. Patil, S. Kotz, and J. K. Ord, Eds., Reidel Publishing Company, Dordrecht and Boston, 1975, pp. 369-384.

Zelen, M., "Problems in the Early Detection of Disease and the Finding of Faults," *Bulletin of the International Statistical Institute,* Vol. 38, 1971, pp. 649-661.

Zelen, M., "Problems in Cell Kinetics and the Early Detection of Disease," in *Reliability and Biometry,* Society for Industrial and Applied Mathematics, 1974, pp. 701-726.

John A. Hendrickson, Jr.,[1] and Richard J. Horwitz[1]

An Overview of Statistical Analysis of Biological Community Data

REFERENCE: Hendrickson, J. A., Jr., and Horwitz, R. J., **"An Overview of Statistical Analysis of Biological Community Data,"** *Statistics in the Environmental Sciences, ASTM STP 845*, S. M. Gertz, Ed., American Society for Testing and Materials, 1984, pp. 23-30.

ABSTRACT: The types of questions usually asked of community data are categorized and used to structure the choice of analyses for any given study. Comments are offered on the relative suitability of various analyses for data acquired in well-designed studies.

KEYWORDS: multivariate analyses, principal components, canonical correlations, cluster analysis, ordination, regression, binary data, multinomial data

In many environmental studies, it is common practice to collect data on the taxonomic composition of each of many samples of plants or animals in the study area. For the moment, we will not be concerned with such details of the design as number of samples and their allocation in space and time; those issues are obviously important in selecting hypotheses of interest and executing the data analysis [1].

We should also immediately concede that we have observational data, rather than data from a fully randomized experiment, with all the implications that distinction has for the questions of correlation versus causation [3,4].

Since our charge in this paper is to consider community structure, we will consider that we have a two-dimensional array, with the rows representing taxa and the columns representing samples. The individual observations in the array may be binary values indicating presence or absence, proportions indicating relative abundance, counts, biomass figures, percent cover, or any of a number of other common biological variables. In addition to the p rows for taxa, there may be q other variables for each column indicating physical, chemical, or habitat characteristics.

[1] Research associate and assistant curator, Division of Environmental Research, Academy of Natural Sciences, Philadelphia, Pa. 19103

Although one could obviously consider such measures as species diversity for each sample, most techniques for comparing species diversity in multiple samples do not consider the taxonomic composition and do not concern us here; for some comments on diversity measures from multiple samples, an earlier paper [2] is of interest.

It is certainly an understatement that there is confusion over what to do with data gathered in such a table [1,5] or whether and how to gather such data, and our purpose is to try to put some organization into the subject.

To begin, we ought to pose some questions about the purpose of our analyses.

1. Are we posing hypotheses about particular species or about community structure?

2. Can we predict, a priori, that certain samples differ in a specific direction?

3. How many groups of samples should we recognize as communities, and which groups?

4. How repeatable are our choices of groups over time and over different choices of analyses? Do these communities appear to have a real structure with defined discontinuities?

5. Do the groups correlate with environmental variables?

It seems worthwhile to pose these questions in the logical structure of a flow-chart, with the ordering of the questions being based on our perceptions of the specifiable objectives of most environmental studies. After considering the question sequence, we will take up individual cases.

Cases

If we are concerned with the response of individual species to the environment, we are not concerned with analyses of the community data as a whole, and hence we go to Case 1.

If we have only one environmental variable of interest, the community analysis is usually straight forward, and we go to Case 2.

If, however, we wish to correlate community structure with many environmental variables simultaneously, we need some advanced techniques considered in Case 3.

If there are a priori contrasts among samples, we are in a test situation, which we consider in Case 4.

If we want to summarize community structure in one or a few dimension(s) based on species covariation, we should consider techniques from Case 5.

If we want an optimal division of the samples into some specified number of groups, we should consider techniques in Case 6.

If we are primarily interested in locating mutually nearest neighbors in species space among the samples, cluster analyses in Case 7 are an option for consideration.

If none of these cases is of interest, either we missed presenting an important question or the study objectives are not well-defined with respect to available techniques.

We will now briefly take up the individual cases.

Case 1—Interest in Particular Species

We may want to consider standard analysis of variance or regression approaches [1,6] or special models such as those described by Ginzburg in the present symposium [7]. Data transformation may be necessary. However, we do not have any immediate need for the analysis of the full community data.

Case 2—Community Structure on a Single Environmental Variable

The most obvious technique here is direct gradient analysis [8, 9]. This is primarily a graphic technique, not associated with any specific underlying model, and, if the interpretation is simple, we usually accept that the idea is helpful. If the interpretation is not obvious, we need to reject the idea and perhaps consider Case 5 or 6.

Case 3—Correlation of Community Structure with Many Environmental Variables

Canonical analysis (often termed canonical correlation analysis) is the collection of techniques for our p community variables and our q environmental variables, using the environmental variables to predict the community variables. The most comprehensive reference for environmental studies is Ref 10.

If the total number of variables is less than the number of observations and there are no missing data, we can usually avoid computational difficulties. While the interpretation of the canonical variates is somewhat more complex than multiple regression, there is perhaps less tendency for misinterpretation of the coefficients to occur. Reference 10 provides a number of worked examples, as well as extensive comments on the problems caused by outliers among the environmental variables. There is probably more need for preliminary analysis with these techniques than with most other multivariate methods used for data description.

Case 4—A priori Contrasts Among Samples

These are all cases in which we can define a sum of squares for heterogeneity among samples and then partition the sum of squares to reflect the contrast or hierarchy of contrasts to be considered. If the contrasts being tested are not orthogonal, the issue of statistical dependence among tests must be considered, but recent discussions indicate that it may not be so major a problem as has long been suggested.

We should briefly address these by types of data. For binary data, the variables in tests are usually the column sums (numbers of species per sample) or the inner products of pairs of columns (numbers of species in common to pairs of samples). For the first, Cochran's Q statistic [11–13] is usually appropriate, while, for the second, a statistic called M is available [12,13]. Although recent workers [14–16] have proposed tests analogous to M but conditional on the column sums (as well as the row sums), these are all seriously flawed by inefficient and biased estimation and testing procedures. Work in progress has defined some exact and approximate tests to replace M with a test conditional on both the row and column sums. If one wishes to condition only on the total number of occurrences of all species, a test statistic for unequal probability of occurrence is given [17].

For relative abundance data, expressed as number of individuals of a given species in the given sample, the most plausible approach is to compute X^2 for hetergeneity among columns, [6] with the understanding that we do not expect X^2 to have a chi-squared distribution since we do not expect a common underlying multinomial distribution in most cases. However, if X^2 is smaller than the critical value for chi-squared with the appropriate degrees of freedom, we clearly do not have any basis to reject a common multinomial distribution and hence we should not reject any related null hypothesis. If X^2 is partitioned and yields a large element associated with the contrast, we should perform a randomization test over the set of equal-sized contrasts within the subset of data being tested, and reject our null hypothesis if this is a significantly large contrast within the randomization set [18]. We are nearly certain that this introduces some conservative bias into such a test, but it is the best procedure among the data-based options, and we find it preferable to a Bayesian specification of an alternative to the common multinomial.

For other data types, the observations or transformed observations may approach multivariate normality sufficiently to permit using multivariate analysis of variance in some of the forms described in Ref 19. Interpretation of results should be tempered by the comments of one reviewer of that book [20] as well as by recent discussion on analysis of studies conducted in the presence of autocorrelations of unknown magnitude [21]. Certainly those remarks apply to any environmental studies, and they bear out earlier comments on the difficulty of designing studies [1,22].

Case 5—Description of a Few Dimensions of the Data, Based on Species Covariances

For binary data, we think we are currently without suitable methods. Some authors have advocated standardization by rows followed by principal components analyses (or factor analysis) of the correlation matrix (referenced in [23]), but this has been widely criticized for both methods and results [24,25]. In particular, the factor estimates do not have interpretable relationships to the covariance structure [25]. Principal coordinate analysis has been proposed as one alternative [24], but we know of only one application of the method to community data. There has recently been a tentative approach to extracting the first factor from logit or probit transformed binary data [25], and the results do have some intuitive appeal. However, the method has not been extended to more than one dimension and, hence, cannot yet be recommended here.

For other types of data, principal components analysis, followed by plotting the sample in the space defined by the first few axes is the eventual method of choice. Before getting to that point, however, there are usually steps involving centering the observations and rescaling the observations. These are inherently biological decisions on how to weight the data; some guidelines, as well as a description of principal components analysis, are given in Ref 26. Since the purpose of such an analysis is not the reconstruction of an environmental gradient through indirect analyses, it is our opinion that we need not be concerned with the difficulties encountered in recovering nonlinear species responses to environmental gradients [27,28]; the intepretation given to the analysis should be clear on this point. It is worth noting that principal components analysis works as a data summarization tool without regard for the normality of the data; such techniques as tests for the uniqueness of eigenvalues, however, are inappropriate unless one satisfies such assumptions as multivariate normality [5].

Case 6—Optimal Division of Samples Into k *Groups*

In principle we can let k be an arbitrary integer, not less than two and not as large as the number of samples. In practice we usually have some idea from other studies as to how many groups are likely to be useful. It is a vastly more difficult problem to find an optimal number of groups and then to seek the optimal division into groups. (This case differs from discriminant analysis in that the assignment of samples to groups is not an input to the analysis but a result of the optimization procedure.)

For binary data, association analysis [29,30] is clearly the method of choice and has a long history of application, particularly in the British and Australian literature. An ad hoc technique in a recent paper [31] appears to provide a crude approximation to the results from association analysis, but the formal technique seems clearly preferable.

For other data, we again must select and apply any centering and scaling techniques before proceeding to a principal components analysis from which we need only to plot the data along the axis corresponding to the first principal component. We then use an optimal decision algorithm for k groups [32]. This is currently the preferred approach to generating groups with minimum within-group heterogeneity and maximum separations within a single dimension.

Case 7—Clustering Mutually Nearest Neighbors

We have come, at last, to the group of techniques which is probably most used in the literature, and certainly all too often used in lieu of Cases 2, 4, 5, or 6.

By its very nature, cluster analysis distorts all patterns except mutually nearest neighbors. It has long been known that cluster analysis does not test hypotheses about which samples are different either by inclusion within a cluster or exclusion from a cluster [*33*]. Groups formed by cluster analysis usually differ from groups formed by optimal divisions, since cluster analysis, at least in its hierarchical forms, does not maximize within-group homogeneity, nor can it do so in general [*34*]. Similarly cluster analysis does not provide an ordering along a single gradient, and even a Prim-network, constructed from single linkage clustering, does not ordinarily provide a strict ordering.

Cluster analysis involves two steps, namely, selection and calculation of an index and subsequent clustering of the matrix of indices. The clustering can be by any of a large number of algorithms, most of which proceed pairwise. (There are other kinds of algorithms, for example, direct, which have not been applied to environmental studies. The interested reader can find many of these in Ref *35* and a recent addition in Ref *36*.) The choice of clustering method influences the kinds of distortion created and the ambiguities which arise in interpreting the resulting diagrams. Some useful references are [*23, 26,* and *37*].

The remaining issue in Case 7 is that of a similarity index. There are many available, as a brief perusal of Refs *23, 26, 37,* and *38* will attest. To be suitably brief, we can consider the more frequently used indices for each data type.

For binary data, it has long been accepted that an index should exclude negative matches from the numerator. There is some discussion over the exclusion of negative matches from the denominator [*36,38*]. The usual indices are either Jaccard or Sorensen, both of which exclude negative matches from the denominator, or Russell and Rao, which uses the total number of species as the denominator for all pairs.

For relative abundance data, the percent similarity index is probably the best known, followed by Morisita's index, which is scaled by the diversity of both samples. The properties of these indices are considered in Refs *39* and *40*.

For other data, indices commonly include correlation coefficients and Euclidean distances, neither of which is a 0 to 1 similarity measure. Their properties are well known.

In particular for binary data, the question has been repeatedly raised as to how much the cluster analysis is determined by the marginal sums of the data table. An approach to this question has been offered in Ref *41*, and some ongoing work may simplify the calculations involved.

Discussion

We need to consider whether the present selection of questions and cases is adequate for environmental studies now being conducted. We welcome your feedback on that.

The question has repeatedly been raised [1,5,10,22] as to whether the data gathered in environmental studies warrant extensive analyses. If the data are gathered with care under a well-chosen design, we think this answer can be affirmative.

The literature is chaotic, but we hope we have found a suitable arrangement of questions and approaches to offer guidance in performing and reviewing analyses of community structure in environmental studies. Perhaps we can view the symposium as a success if we have merely focused our discussions on when to use the methods we do understand.

References

[1] Fritz, E. S., Rago, P. J., and Murarka, I. P. "Strategy for Assessing Impacts of Power Plants on Fish and Shellfish Populations," FWS/OBS-80/34, U.S. Fish and Wildlife Service, Biological Services Program, National Power Plant Team, 1980.

[2] Hendrickson, J. A., Jr., in *Ecological Diversity in Theory and Practice*, J. F. Grassle, G. P. Patil, Woollcott, S., and C. Taillie, eds., International Co-operative Publishing House, Fairland, Md., 1979, pp. 145–158.

[3] Selvin, H. C. and Stuart, A., *American Statistician*, Vol. 20, 1966, pp. 20–23.

[4] Kempthorne, O., *Biometrics*, Vol. 34, 1978, pp. 1–23.

[5] Greig-Smith, P., *Vegetatio*, Vol. 42, 1980, pp. 1–9.

[6] Sokal, R. R. and Rohlf, F. J., *Biometry*, W. H. Freeman and Co., San Francisco, 1981, pp. 1–859.

[7] Ginzburg, L. R. et al, this symposium, pp. 31–45.

[8] Whittaker, R. H., *Ecological Monographs*, Vol. 26, 1956, pp. 1–80.

[9] Whittaker, R. H., *Ecological Monographs*, Vol. 30, 1960, pp. 279–338.

[10] Gittins, R. in *Multivariate Methods in Ecological Works*, L. Orloci, C. R. Rao, and W. M. Stiteler, eds., International Co-operative Publishing House, Fairland, Md., 1979, pp. 309–535.

[11] Cochran, W. G., *Biometrika*, Vol. 37, 1950, pp. 256–266.

[12] Hendrickson, J. A., Jr., in *Biological Data in Water Pollution Assessment: Quantitative and Statistical Analyses, ASTM STP 652*, K. L. Dickson, John Cairns, Jr., and R. J. Livingston, eds., American Society for Testing and Materials, Philadelphia, Pa., 1978, pp. 113–124.

[13] Hendrickson, J. A., Jr., in *Contemporary Quantitative Ecology and Related Ecometrics*, G. P. Patil and M. L. Rosenzweig, eds., International Co-operative Publishing House, Fairland, Md., 1979, pp. 361–397.

[14] Connor, E. S. and Simberloff, D. S., *Ecology*, Vol. 60, 1980, pp. 1132–1140.

[15] Diamond, J. M. and Gilpin, M. E., *Oecologia*, Vol. 52, 1982, pp. 64–74.

[16] Gilpin, M. E. and Diamond, J. M., *Oecologia*, Vol. 52, 1982, pp. 75–84.

[17] Barton, D. E. and David, F. N., *Journal of the Royal Statistical Society, Series B*, Vol. 21, 1959, pp. 190–194.

[18] Bradley, J. V., *Distribution-Free Statistical Tests*, Prentice-Hall, Englewood Cliffs, N.J., 1968, pp. 68–86.

[19] Green, R. H., *Sampling Design and Statistical Method for Environmental Biologists*, Wiley, New York, 1979, pp. 1–257.

[20] Brown, K. G., *Journal of the American Statistical Association*, Vol. 75, 1980, pp. 476–477.

[21] Finney, D. J., *Biometrics*, Vol. 38, 1982, pp. 255–267.

[22] Eberhardt, L. L., *Journal of Environmental Management*, Vol. 4, 1976, pp. 22–70.

[23] Sneath, P. H. A. and Sokal, R. R., *Numerical Taxonomy*, W. H. Freeman and Co., San Francisco, Cal., 1973, pp. 1–573.

[24] Gower, J. C., *Biometrika*, Vol. 53, 1966, pp. 325–338.

[25] Bartholomew, D. J., *Journal of the Royal Statistical Society, Series B*, Vol. 42, 1980, pp. 293–321.

[26] Orloci, L., *Multivariate Analysis in Vegetation Research*, 2nd edition, W. Junk, The Hague, 1978.

[27] Van der Maarel, *Vegetatio*, Vol. 42, 1980, pp. 43–45.

[28] Gauch, H. G., Jr., *Multivariate Analysis in Community Ecology*, Cambridge University Press, New York, 1982, pp. 1–298.

[29] Williams, W. T. and Lambert, J. M., *Journal of Ecology*, Vol. 47, 1959, pp. 83–101.

[30] Williams, W. T. and Lambert, J. M., *Journal of Ecology*, Vol. 48, 1960, pp. 689–710.

[31] Strahler, A. H., *Ecology*, Vol. 59, 1978, pp. 108–116.

[32] Noy-Meir, Imanuel, *Journal of Ecology*, Vol. 61, 1973, pp. 753–760.

[33] Cormack, R. M., *Journal of the Royal Statistical Society, Series A*, Vol. 134, 1971, pp. 321–367.

[34] Rubin, Jerrold, *Systematic Zoology*, Vol. 15, 1966, pp. 169–182.

[35] Hartigan, J. A., *Clustering Algorithms*, Wiley, New York, 1975, pp. 1–336.

[36] Buser, M. W. and Baroni-Urbani, C., *Biometrics*, Vol. 38, 1982, pp. 351–360.

[37] Clifford, H. T. and Stephenson, W., *An Introduction to Numerical Classification*, Academic Press, New York, 1975.

[38] Goodall, D. W. in *Handbook of Vegetation Science*, R. Tuxen, ed., Part V., W. Junk, The Hague, 1973, pp. 105–156.

[39] Smith, W., Kravitz, D., and Grassle, J. F. in *Multivariate Methods in Ecological Work*, L. Orloci, C. R. Rao, and W. M. Stiteler, eds., International Co-operative Publishing House, Fairland, Md., 1979, pp. 253–262.

[40] Smith, E. P. and Zaret, T. M., *Ecology*, Vol. 63, 1982, pp. 1248–1253.

[41] Strauss, R. E., *Ecology*, Vol. 63, 1982, pp. 634–639.

Lev R. Ginzburg, [1] *Keith Johnson,* [2] *Andrea Pugliese,* [3] *and John Gladden,* [4]

Ecological Risk Assessment Based on Stochastic Age-Structured Models of Population Growth

REFERENCE: Ginzburg, L. R., Johnson, K., Pugliese, A., and Gladden, J., "**Ecological Risk Assessment Based on Stochastic Age-Structures Models of Population Growth,**" *Statistics in the Environmental Sciences, ASTM STP 845,* S. M. Gertz and M. D. London, Eds., American Society for Testing and Materials, 1984, pp. 31–45.

ABSTRACT: A method is developed to evaluate the risk of a population crossing a preassigned critical level in a given period of time. The method is based on the stochastic age-structured model of population dynamics. The two-step process is suggested. The first step constructs the "effective" one-dimensional model with the autocorrelated noise term reflecting the underlying multidimensional process. The second step solves the first passage time problem in a one-dimensional context.

KEY WORDS: environment, risk assessment, stochastic models, age-structure, population growth, first passage

In a previous paper [1] we argued for the assessment of the risk of quasiextinction (that is, population size crossing of a low preassigned level) as a useful way to quantify the concept of environmental impact on natural populations. The practical realization of the suggested approach requires estimating the finite time first passage probability for a set of special stochastic processes which represent the dynamics of the populations in question. This paper suggests a possible methodology based on stochastic age-structured models of population

[1]Professor, Department of Ecology and Evolution, State University of New York at Stony Brook, Stony Book, N.Y. 11794.
[2]Analytics Ind., Tinton Falls, N.J. 07724.
[3]Graduate student, Department of Ecology and Evolution, State University of New York at Stony Brook, Stony Brook, N.Y. 11794.
[4]Savannah River Ecology Laboratory, Aiken, S.C. 29801.

31

growth. An example based on the data for the Hudson River striped bass population shows the effectiveness and limitations of the suggested method.

Let us start with the description of the underlying model. This is the standard Leslie matrix model [2] which has already been used in a variety of applications. The major difference is that we allow the elements of the matrix, which are fertilities and survivals for different age groups, to be stationary stochastic processes rather than constants as in the traditional model. To simplify our consideration, we assume as in Ref 3 that the only stochastically varying parameter is the juvenile survival. This assumption is reasonable for the example which we will develop and is a biologically sound intermediate step between fully deterministic and fully stochastic life-history description. The reason is that, as a rule, early stages of life are most vulnerable with respect to environmental changes, and, therefore, the variability in juvenile survival is much greater than variability in fertility values or adult survival.

The model, therefore is simply a recurrent system of linear equations

$$X_{t+1} = A_t X_t \tag{1}$$

where

t = discrete time, $t = 0, 1, \ldots,$

X_t = vector of abundances of n different age groups $(x_{it}, \ldots, x_{nt})$,

A_t = Leslie matrix of the form

$$
A_t =
\begin{vmatrix}
0 & f_1 & f_2 & \cdots & f_{n-1} & f_n \\
p_0(t) & 0 & 0 & \cdots & 0 & 0 \\
0 & p_1 & 0 & \cdots & 0 & 0 \\
0 & 0 & p_2 & \cdots & 0 & 0 \\
\cdot & \cdot & \cdot & \cdot & \cdot & \cdot \\
0 & 0 & 0 & \cdots & p_{n-1} & 0
\end{vmatrix}
\tag{2}
$$

where f_i represents fertilities of the females of the ith age and p_i represents the survival between ages $(i - 1)$ and i. The only stochastically varying parameter is the matrix is $p_0(t)$. Let us note from the very beginning that this assumption is in no way a limitation to the suggested method. The method will work with all the fertilities and survival being stochastic with arbitrary covariation structure. We have chosen to work with this special model in order to simplify our formulations. In practice, the use of more general models involving stochasticity in more or even all parameters is limited much more severely by the available data rather than mathematical technicalities. This does not mean that the problem is mathematically simple. We consider the difficulties of solving it next. However, most of the mathematical difficulties encountered are already contained in the simplified version [2], and we felt that the idea of our approach would be only obscured by overgeneralizations.

In applications we are usually interested in a particular scalar variable, like the abundance of adults, juveniles, or any specific subgroup of a population. It may be also a biomass of a subgroup or any other variable of interest which is a linear combination of the original age group abundances. Let us denote this variable as N

$$N(t) = (b, X_t) = \sum_{i=1}^{n} b_i x_{it} \tag{3}$$

The choice of the vector b is dictated by purely practical consideration and has no relation to the population dynamics. If $b = (1, \ldots, 1)$ $N(t)$ will represent, for instance, the total population size at time t, and, if $b = (0, 1, \ldots, 1)$, $N(t)$ will be the abundance of juveniles.

An important asymptotic property of the process X_t has been established under a set of biologically nonrestrictive assumptions about the parameters in Eq 2 [4,5]. It does not make sense to repeat these assumptions here, the interested reader is referred to the original papers.

This property is that asymptotically vector X_t is approximately lognormally distributed. In other words, there exist two constants, a and σ such that

$$\frac{\ln(b, X_t) - at}{\sigma\sqrt{t}} \to Y \tag{4}$$

where Y is the standard normal variable with zero mean and variance equal to 1. The convergence is in distribution. It is particularly important that constants a and σ are independent of b. In other words, any variable of interest, $N(t)$, as defined in Eq 3 with different vectors b is asymptotically equally and lognormally distributed.

This result gives us the possibility to evaluate the risks of the population variable $N(t)$ falling below a given critical level, N_c, at the time t as

$$\text{prob}\left[N(t) \leq N_c\right] \approx \Phi\left(\frac{\ln N_c - at}{\sigma\sqrt{t}}\right) \tag{5}$$

where

$$\Phi(y) = \frac{1}{\sqrt{2\pi}} \int_{-\infty}^{y} e^{\frac{\zeta^2}{2}} \, d\zeta$$

Equation 5 is valid, certainly, only if t is large enough. For one-dimensional models, this formula works for all t. Since we consider it as an approximation for a more complex multidimensional process, the actual time depends on the initial age distribution. Practically, a few generation times are sufficient for the Eq 5 to be quite accurate. Thus, in some sense, the problem of the long-term risk evaluation is resolved as long as we are able to evaluate parameters a and σ. Formulae for the approximate evaluation of these two parameters were developed in Ref 5.

The more difficult, but practically much more relevant, question is the evaluation of the probability that $N(t)$ will cross the level N_c at *least once* in a given period of time, or

$$\text{prob}\left[\min_{0 \leq \tau \leq t} N(\tau) \leq N_c\right] \qquad (6)$$

This is the problem that we discuss next. We approach the problem in two steps. First, we build the one-dimensional "effective" model which asymptotically simulates the behavior of the underlying age-structured model; then, we consider a one-dimensional first-passage time problem in terms of the variable $N(t)$.

"Effective" One-Dimensional Model

The fundamental asymptotic property cited previously and, particularly the independence of a and σ of the vector b, suggests that it might be possible to develop a one-dimensional model for the variable of interest, $N(t)$, in the form

$$N_{t+1} = (a + \zeta_{t+1})N(t) \qquad (7)$$

where ζ is a zero-mean stationary process with some autocorrelation structure. Although a and σ are independent of the vector b, we will see that the autocorrelation structure will depend strongly on the choice of this vector. We, therefore, have very different "effective" one-dimensional models for different definitions of the variable N. For every specific choice of b, however, the one-dimensional model behaves asymptotically as the underlying multidimensional process, and we can attempt to use the simpler model to estimate desired probabilities. Note that the process $\zeta(t)$ will be autocorrelated even if we assume the original process $p_0(t)$ to be uncorrelated. The autocorrelation is borne by the underlying age-structured multidimensional model. Nothing prevents us from assuming that environmental fluctuations, and, therefore, the juvenile survival, $p_0(t)$, have a particular autocorrelation structure, too. The resulting autocorrelation function for $\zeta(t)$ will then depend on, environmentally induced historic influences, the Leslie matrix parameters, and the choice of the variable of interest, b. In order to simplify notations let us assume the environmental fluctuations to be of the "white noise" type, that is, $p_0(t)$ is the process with zero autocorrelations. All the calculations can be generalized to include environmentally induced correlations if necessary.

To present our results we will need to introduce new notations and assumptions. We assume that

$$A_t = \bar{A} + B_t \tag{8}$$

where $E(B_t) = 0$ and higher moments are "small." In our case this just means that

$$p_0(t) = \bar{p} + \Delta p(t) \tag{9}$$

and the coefficient of variation for Δp is small. We will use a special notation for this coefficient of variation

$$(cv)^2 = \frac{\text{variance}(\Delta p)}{\bar{p}^2} \tag{10}$$

Then, let us introduce notations for the eigenvectors and eigenvalues of the mean matrix, $\bar{A}$. We will use λ for the dominant eigenvalue and u and v for the corresponding left and right eigenvectors. All the other eigenvalues will be numbered: $\lambda_2, \ldots, \lambda_n$ with the corresponding left and right eigenvectors $u_2, \ldots, u_n$ and $v_2, \ldots, v_n$.

Omitting the calculations which are sketched in the Appendix, we will present the results. One additional assumption has been made here in order to simplify our expressions: $X_0 = v$. The population structure will be close to v if it has grown with the Leslie matrix $\bar{A}$ for a long enough time. This assumption, again, is not restrictive. The same computations can be repeated with any initial age structure.

$$E[\ell n N(t)] \simeq t \ell n \lambda + \ell n(b, v) - \frac{t(cv)^2}{2(u, v)^2} + \frac{(cv)^2}{2(b, v)^2} \Sigma_{\alpha, \beta \neq (1,1)}$$

$$\times \frac{(b, v_\alpha)(b, v_\beta) \lambda_\alpha \lambda_\beta}{(u_\alpha, v_\alpha)(u_\beta, u_\beta)(\lambda^2 - \lambda_\alpha \lambda_\beta)} \left[1 - \left(\frac{\lambda_\alpha \lambda_\beta}{\lambda^2} \right)^t \right] \tag{11}$$

$$\text{cov}(\ell n N(t+k), \ell n N(t)) \simeq t \frac{(CV)^2}{(u, v)^2} + \frac{(CV)^2}{\lambda^k(b, v)^2} \Sigma_{\alpha, \beta \neq (1,1)}$$

$$\times \frac{(b, v_\alpha)(b, v_\beta) \lambda_\alpha \lambda_\beta^{k+1}}{(u_\alpha, v_\alpha)(u_\beta, u_\beta)(\lambda^2 - \lambda_\alpha \lambda_\beta)} \left[1 - \left(\frac{\lambda_\alpha \lambda_\beta}{\lambda^2} \right)^t \right] \tag{12}$$

As

$$a = \lim_{t \to \infty} E\left[\frac{\ell n N(t)}{t} \right] \quad \text{and} \quad \sigma^2 = \lim_{t \to \infty} \frac{\text{variance}[\ell n N(t)]}{t}$$

One finds from Eq 11 and Eq 12 approximate expressions for a and σ

$$a \simeq \ell n \lambda - \frac{(CV)^2}{2(u,v)^2} \quad \text{and} \quad \sigma^2 \simeq \frac{(CV)^2}{(u^1 v)^2} \tag{13}$$

as in Ref 5.

Moreover, from Eqs 11 and 12 one finds also variance and autocorrelation of the increments as

$$V\left[\ell n N(t+1) - \ell n N(t)\right] \simeq \frac{(CV)^2}{(u,v)^2} + \frac{(CV)^2}{(b,v)^2} \Sigma_{\beta \neq 1} \Sigma_\alpha$$

$$\times \frac{(b,v_\alpha)(b,v_\beta)\lambda_\alpha\lambda_\beta}{(u_\alpha,v_\alpha)(u_\beta,v_\beta)(\lambda^2 - \lambda_\alpha\lambda_\beta)}\left(1 - \frac{\lambda_\beta}{\lambda}\right) \tag{14}$$

and

$$\text{cov}(\ell n N(t+k+1) - \ell n N(t+k), \ell n N(t+1) - \ell n N(t)) \simeq - \frac{(CV)^2}{(b,v)^2}$$

$$\times \Sigma_{\beta \neq 1}\Sigma_\alpha \frac{(b,v_\alpha)(b,v_\beta)\lambda_\alpha\lambda_\beta}{(u_\alpha,v_\alpha)(u_\beta,v_\beta)(\lambda^2 - \lambda_\alpha\lambda_\beta)}\left(1 - \frac{\lambda_\beta}{\lambda}\right)^2\left(\frac{\lambda_\beta}{\lambda}\right)^{k-1} \quad \text{for} \quad k \geq 1 \tag{15}$$

The question of the accuracy of the suggested approximations naturally appears at this point. How small should the CV be for this approximation to hold? We do not have the general answer to this question. The procedure leading to the formulae given previously can be repeated retaining higher moments of $B(t)$. We have done that and carried out numerical simulations for a number of Leslie matrices. Our experience was that for the standard deviation of P_0 up to about 75%, the results for a and σ^2 are quite accurate.

First-Passage Time Problem

Assuming that our one-dimensional model approximates the "real" multidimensional process closely enough, we are left with the problem of quasi-extinction for a one-dimensional process. To our knowledge, there are no general results for this problem. However, for a continuous time process with *independent increments*, say, $Y(t)$ with infinitesimal drift and variance a and σ^2, respectively, it is well known [7] that the probability of first crossing the boundary y between time t and $t + dt$, conditional to $Y(0) = x$, is given by

$$f(t,x,y)\,dt = \frac{[x-y]}{(2\pi\sigma^2 t)^{1/2}t} \exp\left[-\frac{(x-y+at)^2}{2\sigma^2 t}\right] dt \tag{16}$$

The mean and variance of $Y(t)$ are

$$E(t) = E[Y(t)] = at \qquad V(t) = V[Y(t)] = \sigma^2 t$$

so that we can rewrite Eq 16 in terms of these notations as

$$f(t,x,y) = \frac{[x - y] V^1(t)}{[2\pi V(t)]^{1/2} V(t)} \exp\left[-\frac{(x - y + E(t))^2}{2V(t)} \right] \qquad (17)$$

We accepted this formula as the valid generalization of the classical result applicable for the autocorrelated case. To account for the discrete nature of the process we considered, we used (Eq 17, multiplied by time step 1) as the probability of first crossing at time unit t. Although we were able to prove this result only for special cases, we have checked it numerically for a number of simple autocorrelated processes including exponential autocorrelation and one-time correlation. In our case, $Y(t)$ corresponds to $\ell n\, N(t)$, and the variance-covariance structure of its increments is described in Eqs 14 and 15. Using them, and basic probability formulae, we computed a theoretical mean and variance of $\ell n\, N(t)$, which we substituted in Eq 17 for $E(t)$ and $V(t)$. Also x was set equal to $\ell n\, N_0$ and y to $\ell n\, N_c$. Finally, we summed Eq 17 for all times up to t, to have the probability of crossing N_c at least once before t.

In all the cases, this formula gave a very good approximation for the real probability when the probability that we estimate is low, that is, either critical level is much lower than the initial or the variability, σ^2, is low or both. Mistakes grow when the estimated probability is high, that is, either critical level is close to the initial or variability is very high or both.

When risks are high, the Monte Carlo simulations will provide the answer reasonably quickly and accurately. It is the problem of low risks that deserves special attention, and our approximation is especially geared towards evaluating small risks. We believe that in most practical applications, the risks are represented by sufficiently low probabilities, say, less than 0.1. In such cases, Eq 17 is an excellent analytic tool to evaluate the desired risk value as defined in the introduction. The two-step approach that we suggest in this paper creates, therefore, a useful analytic-numerical method of risk analysis that can replace the straightforward Monte Carlo simulations.

Example

To test our method we have carried out extensive Monte Carlo simulations representing "natural" behavior of the stochastic age-structured growth process. We have estimated risks based on these simulations to generate the "true" values. Then we applied our method to the same problem to see whether the true results can be predicted analytically. A certain amount of numerical work is necessary to generate the theoretical predictions. This is chiefly to calculate all the eigenvalues of the mean Leslie matrix, $\bar{A}$. Eigenvectors for this special matrix are very easy to compute, and all the other calculations are just summations of the corresponding terms in the approximate expressions for the $E[\ell n\, N(t)]$ and cov $[\ell n\, N(t+k),\, \ell n\, N(t)]$.

The other issue which should be discussed here is the choice of critical levels. In the density-independent model which we consider here it is natural to choose critical levels in terms of a percentage of the initial level. This is the way we did it in a one-dimensional context [1]. In the age-structured context depending on the variable of interest, $N(t)$, the "effective" initial level of this variable should be assigned so that the critical levels are computed as the percentages of it. We can choose this effective level based on the behavior of the mean model

$$X_{t+1} = \bar{A}X_t \qquad (18)$$

The general solution of this system is

$$X_t = \gamma_1 V\gamma^t + \sum_{k=2}^{n} \gamma_k v_k \lambda_k^t \qquad (19)$$

where $\gamma_1, \ldots, \gamma_n$ are coefficients depending on the initial condition, X_0. The expression for these coefficients in terms of X_0 is well-known. We will need only the formula for γ_1

$$\gamma_1 = \frac{(u, X_0)}{(u, v)} \qquad (20)$$

Now, with the choice of our variable of interest (vector b) we have

$$N(t) = (b, X_t) = \gamma_2(b, v)\lambda^t + \sum_{k=2}^{n} \gamma_k(b, v_k)\lambda_k^t \qquad (21)$$

Since $|\lambda_k| < \lambda$ we have when $t \to \infty$

$$N(t) \approx \gamma_1(b, v) \cdot \lambda^t \qquad (22)$$

If we want our "effective" one-dimensional model to resemble asymptotically the behavior of the underlying age-structured model we should choose, therefore, the initial level $N(o) = \gamma_1(b, v)$ or

$$N(o) = \frac{(u, X_0)}{(u, v)} (b, v) \qquad (23)$$

We have chosen to do our comparison of the theory and Monte Carlo simulations on the specific example of the Hudson River striped bass. This is one of the hardest cases for the theory since the age distribution is very broad (bass live for at least 20 years) and asymptotic considerations require very long simulations. We took the parameters for the Leslie matrix as they were estimated based on data collected by Texas Instrument [10]. The value of the asymptotic rate of increase, λ, resulting from the parameters is 1.0092, so that the population would remain almost stationary if driven by the mean matrix. Consequently, the probability of quasi-extinction will be very sensitive to the choice of the critical level.

A brief description of striped bass life history is given in Appendix II. Since we use these values only as an example for checking out our methodology, the

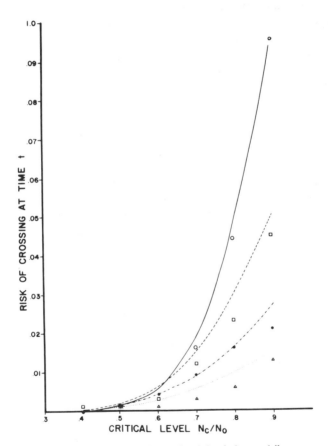

The points correspond to the results of simulations as follows:

$\bigcirc$ = 200
$\square$ = 150
$\bullet$ = 100
$\triangle$ = 50

FIG. 1—*The probabilities of being below the level* N_c *at time* t *as functions of* N_c/N_0 *at various times. The solid lines are computed through Eqs 5 and 13 for* t = 50, 100, 150, *and* 200 *years.*

relevance of these parameters to the actual population is a secondary issue. In general, for the shorter-lived species, our approach will clearly work better because there will be more generations fitted into the same period of time and the trajectory will be closer to its asymptotic behavior.

Let us review some of the results that we obtained for the striped bass model. We have chosen $p_0(t)$ to be a lognormally and independently distributed random variable with $CV = .5$. The variable of interest $N(t)$ was defined as the overall number of adults (ages 5 through 20), so that $b = 0, 0, 0, 0, 1, \ldots, 1$).

First, in Fig. 1 we show the simulated results versus the asymptotic expectation for the probability of falling below a certain level at time t (Eq 5).

In Fig. 2, we show the comparison of the autocorrelation functions for the variable $N(t)$ obtained theoretically versus the one which was reconstructed from simulations. They are clearly in agreement. Basically, we have constant negative correlation for the first four years and a correlation practically indistinguishable from zero for longer intervals of time.

The behavior of the risk of crossing at least once over the period (o, t) is shown in Fig. 3. The theoretical curve agrees with the simulated results quite well. For comparison we also plotted the curve based on the purely "white noise" theory (disregarding the autocorrelation in the $\zeta(t)$ process). The comparison demonstrates that we cannot ignore autocorrelation which is borne by the underlying age-structured process when we try to look at the population growth macroscopically as at a one-dimensional process. At the same time, from the point of view of risk calculation, the autocorrelated one-dimensional model catches the essence of the process quite well.

In practice, the decision of what should be the critical level is quite difficult.

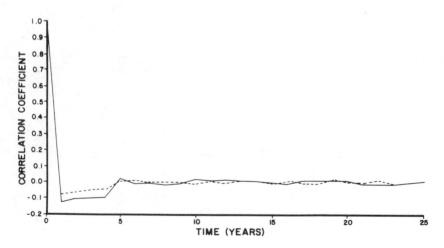

FIG. 2—*The autocorrelation functions for the variable log* $N(t + n + 1) - log\ N(t + n)$ *considered as function of* n, *with* $N(t)$ *defined above. The solid line is computed through Eqs 14 and 15. The broken line is an average over the simulations.*

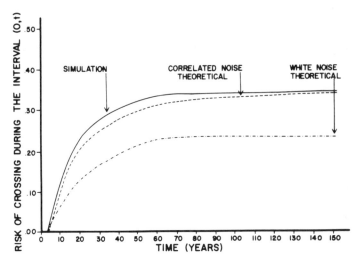

FIG. 3—*The risk of crossing the level* $N_c = 0.8 N_0$ *at least once in the interval* $(0, t)$ *as functions of* t. *The correlated noise curve is computed through Eqs 17, 11, and 12. The white noise is computed through Eqs 16 and 13.*

In any case, this decision lies outside our method. We can only estimate risk given the level. It makes sense, therefore, to present results as a function of the critical level. Figure 4 gives results in this form. Again, we see close agreement between simulated and theoretically estimated results.

Acknowledgments

We would like to express our thanks to Dr. L. Ricciardi (Naples, Italy) and Dr. S. Tuljapurkar (Portland, Oregon) for very useful discussions. This work was supported by Environmental Protection Agency grant number R807885010 to Lev R. Ginzburg and is contribution number 481 from the Department of Ecology and Evolution at the State University of New York at Stony Brook. The conclusions represent the views of the authors and do not necessarily reflect opinions, policies, or recommendations of the Environmental Protection Agency.

APPENDIX I

In order to approximate logarithmic moments of N_t, we employ Tuljapurkar's [6] method of developing the matrix product $A_t \ldots A_1$ in terms of $\bar{A}$ and B_t and discarding the terms where the B_i's matrices are present more than twice.

Moreover, we use the fact that v is a right eigenvector of $\bar{A}$ to yield $\bar{A}^i v = \lambda^i v$, and we use the special shape of the matrices B_t to simplify the expressions. The computations

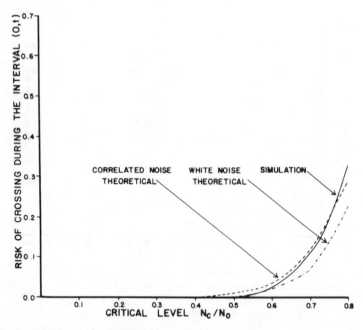

FIG. 4—*The risk of crossing the level* N_c *at least once in the interval* (o, t) *as functions of* N_c/N_0 *at* t $= 50$. *The curves are computed as in Fig. 3.*

work as follows (by v' we mean the transposed of v and by $(A)_n$ where A is a matrix the vector formed by the nth column of A):

$$\ell n\, N_t = \ell n\,(b'\,A_t \ldots A_1 v) \simeq \ell n\,(\lambda^t b'v + \sum_{i=1}^{t} \lambda^{i-1} b'\bar{A}^{t-1} B_i v$$

$$+ \sum_{i=1}^{t-1} \sum_{j=i+1}^{t} \lambda^{i-1} b'\bar{A}^{t-j} B_j \bar{A}^{j-i-1} B_i v)$$

$$\simeq t\,\ell n\,\lambda + \ell n\,(b'v) + \frac{\displaystyle\sum_{i=1}^{t} \lambda^{i-1} \Delta p(i) b'\,(\bar{A}^{t-1})_2}{\lambda^t b'v} \qquad (24)$$

$$+ \frac{\displaystyle\sum_{i=1}^{t-2} \sum_{j=i+2}^{t} \lambda^{i-1} \Delta p(i) \Delta p(j) (\bar{A}^{j-i-1})_{12} b'\,(\bar{A}^{t-j})_2}{\lambda^t b'v}$$

$$+ \frac{\displaystyle\sum_{i=1}^{t} \sum_{j=1}^{t} \lambda^{i-1} \lambda^{j-1} \Delta p(i) \Delta p(j) b'\,(\bar{A}^{t-i})_2 b'\,(\bar{A}^{t-j})_2}{2\lambda^{2t} (b'v)^2}$$

$$\ell n N_t \, \ell n N_{t+k} \simeq (t \, \ell n \, \lambda + \ell n (b'v)) \, \ell n N_{t+k} + ((t+k) \, \ell n \, \lambda + \ell n (b'v)) \, \ell n N_t$$

(25)

$$+ \sum_{i=1}^{t} \sum_{j=1}^{t+k} \frac{\lambda^{i-1} \Delta p(i) b' (\bar{A}^{t-i})_2 \, \lambda^{j-1} \Delta p(j) b' (\bar{A}^{t+k-j})_2}{\lambda^{2t+k} (b'v)^2}$$

By using $E(\Delta p(i)) = 0$ and the independence of $\Delta p(i)$ and $\Delta p(j)$ for $i \neq j$ the third and fourth terms on the right side of Eq 24 need not be considered when taking the mean. Moreover, we use the Jordan form of $\bar{A}$ (assuming that $\bar{A}$ can be diagonalized)

$$\bar{A} = \sum_{\alpha=1}^{n} \frac{\lambda_\alpha}{(u'_\alpha v_\alpha)} v_\alpha u'_\alpha$$

(26)

(λ_1 is the dominant eigenvalue) so that

$$(\bar{A}^{t-i})_2 = \sum_{\alpha=1}^{n} \frac{u_\alpha(2) \lambda_\alpha^{t-i}}{(u'_\alpha v_\alpha)} v_\alpha = \frac{1}{P} \sum_{\alpha=1}^{n} \frac{\lambda_\alpha^{t+1-i}}{(u'_\alpha v_\alpha)} v_\alpha$$

(27)

Using Eq 27 inside Eq 24, together with the previous considerations the opportune rearrangements, yields Eq 11. Equation 12 can be obtained from Eq 25 in the same way. To get Eq 14 and Eq 15 one needs only to expand the left hand side, substitute the appropriate expressions from Eq 12 and discard the terms containing $(\lambda_\alpha/\alpha)^t$ for some $\alpha \neq 1$, that go to zero exponentially with t.

APPENDIX II

Striped Bass Population Characteristics

Striped bass may live for over 20 years. Male Hudson River fish begin to mature at Age II and virtually all males (>90 percent) are sexually mature by Age VII. Female striped bass mature much later with less than 10 percent of Age IV fish found to be sexually mature, but, as with males, the vast majority (>90 percent) are mature by Age VII. The fecundity of sexually mature females in the Hudson River can range from approximately 3×10^5 to 3×10^6 eggs per female. Fecundity is more closely related to fish length or weight than age [8-10] and generally increases with age since growth is indeterminate.

A dominant feature of striped bass population dynamics is a striking variation in the production of young from year to year. Such variations have been observed for years in fishery yield statistics from several different estuarine stocks [11-13]. Since the iteroparous habit of striped bass tends to dampen variations in annual egg production, the large variations in annual cohort size must be a result of variations in the survival of egg, larvae, and juveniles. Boone and Florence [14] have suggested that the major differences in cohort size are determined no later than early juvenile stages.

Direct estimates of juvenile abundance and first year survival have been made in the Hudson River in most years since 1969. During that short span of time, annual juvenile abundance has fluctuated almost six times (minimum to maximum) [10], presumably

TABLE 1—*Population model parameters based on measured Hudson River striped bass population characteristics (females only).*

Age	Probability of Survival	Percent Mature	Effective Fecundity
0	2.9027×10^{-6}	0	0
I	0.3407	0	0
II	0.5571	0	0
III	0.7025	0	0
IV	0.803	4	275500
V	0.803	18	283500
VI	0.803	56	340500
VII	0.803	91	404500
VIII	0.803	100	576500
IX	0.803	100	777000
X	0.803	100	885500
XI	0.803	100	1011000
XII	0.803	100	1120000
XIII	0.803	100	1180000
XIV	0.803	100	1250000
XV	0.803	100	1295500
XVI	0.803	100	1370000
XVII	0.803	100	1440000
XVIII	0.803	100	1509500
XIX	0	100	1509500

as a result of large variations in the survival of eggs, larvae, and early juveniles. Overall first year survival is believed to be on the order of 10^{-5} to 10^{-6} with the greatest mortality associated with eggs and larvae.

The Age Structured Population Model

A Leslie matrix model [7] has been developed that is based on multiple year estimates of the life history parameters of the Hudson River striped bass stock [10]. This model contains twenty age classes (Ages 0 to XIX) and females are considered to begin maturing at Age IV with all females mature by Age VIII (Table 1). Both average individual fecundity and effective fecundity (average fecundity $\times$ percent mature) increase with age. Adult ($\geq$ Age IV) probabilities of survival have been recalculated to reflect an unfished population and are thus somewhat higher than found in most striped bass models [15] that consider total mortality from both natural sources and fishing. Adult survival is considered to remain constant. The probabilities of survival for prereproductive individuals (Age I to III) have also been recalculated based on the estimated abundance of juvenile striped bass in 1973 and 1974 and estimates of Age IV abundance four years later and assuming that survival increases with age.

References

[1] Ginzburg, L. R., Slobodkin, L. B., Johnson, K., and Bindman, A. G., "Quasiextinction Probabilities as a Measure of Impact on Population Growth," *Risk Analysis* (in press).

[2] Leslie, P. H., "On the Use of Matrices in Certain Population Mathematics," *Biometrika*, Vol. 33, pp. 183-212.

[3] O'Neill, R. V., Gardner, R. H., Christensen, S. W., Van Winkle, W., Carney, J. H., and Mankin, J. B., "Some Effects of Parameter Uncertainty in Density-Independent and

Density-Dependent Leslie Models for Fish Populations," *Canadian Journal of Fisheries and Aquatic Sciences*, Vol. 38, pp. 91–100.

[4] Cohen, J. E., "Ergodicity of Age Structure in Populations with Markovian Vital Notes. II. General states," *Advances in Applied Probability*, Vol. 9, pp. 18–37.

[5] Tuljapurkar, S. D. and Orzack, S. H., "Population Dynamics in Variable Environments. I. Long-run Growth Rates and Extinction," *Theoretical Population Biology*, Vol. 18, pp. 314–342.

[6] Tuljapurkar, S. D., "Population Dynamics in Variable Environments. III. Evolutionary Dynamics of r-Selection," *Theoretical Population Biology*, Vol. 21, pp. 141–165.

[7] Capocelli, R. M. and Ricciardi, L. M., "A Diffusion Model for Population Growth in Random Environments," *Theoretical Population Biology*, Vol. 5, pp. 28–41.

[8] Lewis, R. M. and Bonner, R. R., Jr., "Fecundity of the Striped Bass, Roccus saxatilis (Walbaum)," *Transactions of the American Fisheries Society*, Vol. 95, pp. 328–331.

[9] Hardy, J. D., Jr., "Development of Fishes of the Mid-Atlantic Bight: An Atlas of the Egg, Larval and Juvenile Stages. Vol III. Aphredoderidae through Rachycentridae. *U.S. Wildlife Service Program*, FWS/OBS-78/12.

[10] "1979 Year Class Report for the Multiplant Impact Study of the Hudson River Estuary," prepared for Consolidated Edison Co. of New York, Inc. by Texas Instruments Inc., 1981.

[11] Merriman, D., "Studies on the Striped Bass (Roccus saxatilis) of the Atlantic Coast," *Fish Bulletin*, U.S. Fisheries and Wildlife Services, Vol. 50, pp. 1–77.

[12] Raney, E. C., "The Striped Bass in New York Waters," *Conservationist*, Vol. 8, pp. 14–17.

[13] Koo, T. S. Y., The striped bass fishery in the Atlantic states, *Chesapeake Sciences*, Vol. 11, pp. 73–93.

[14] Boone, J. G. and Florence, B. M., "The Status of Striped Bass and Maryland's Role in the Fortunes of This Valuable Fish," Maryland Department of Natural Resource Fisheries Administration, 1977.

[15] Swartzman, G. L., Deriso, R. B., and Cowan, C., "Comparison of Simulation Models Used in Assessing the Effects of Power-Plant Induced Mortality of Fish Populations," prepared for U.S. Nuclear Regulatory Commission, NURE6/CR-0474, UW-NRC-10, 1978.

H. Daniel Roth,[1] *Ronald E. Wyzga,*[2] *and*
Thomas Hammerstrom[3]

The Use of Risk Assessment in Developing Health-Based Regulations

REFERENCE: Roth, H. D., Wyzga, R. E., and Hammerstrom, T., **"The Use of Risk Assessment in Developing Health-Based Regulations,"** *Statistics in the Environmental Sciences, ASTM STP 845,* S. M. Gertz and M. D. London, Eds., American Society for Testing and Materials, 1984, pp. 46–65.

ABSTRACT: The six major steps in risk assessment are defined. Difficulties arising in each of the steps are discussed. The use of risk assessment by Federal regulatory agencies is briefly surveyed, and some recent legislation mandating risk assessment is listed.

KEY WORDS: risk assessment, dose-response curves, extrapolation, epidemiological studies, animal toxicological studies, human laboratory studies, health-based regulations

The purpose of this paper is to give an overview of strategies being employed to develop environmental health-based regulations for air and water quality. In the past, regulations were designed so that for all segments of the population the risk, defined as the increase above background in the incidence rate of specified harmful effects, would be zero. The new strategy for developing regulations calls for assessing the risks associated with varying levels of pollution and setting standards at levels which provide reasonable protection to the general public. Standards based on the risk assessment approach are frequently more defensible from both a scientific and a cost-benefit standpoint than ones based on a zero-risk approach.

The paper is divided into four sections: (1) an overview of the general steps involved in performing risk assessment; (2) a discussion of the difficulties associated with each of these steps; (3) a status report of the current use of risk

---

[1]President, Roth Associates, Inc., Rockville, Md. 20852.
[2]Technical manager of Environmental Risk Analyses, Energy Analyses and Environmental Division, Electric Power Research Institute, Palo Alto, Calif. 94303.
[3]Senior statistician, Roth Associates, Inc., Rockville, Md. 20852.

assessment in developing health-based regulations; and (4) a discussion of legislative activities regarding risk assessment.

Major Steps and Issues in Performing Risk Assessment

The goal of risk assessment is to provide point and interval estimates for the increase (or decrease) in the incidence rate of a specified health effect to be expected as the result of a given increase (respectively decrease) in the amount of a specific pollutant in the atmosphere or water. Figure 1 outlines the general steps considered desirable in performing a risk assessment although steps 1, 5, and 6 are often omitted in practice. Those include:

1. Identification and characterization of high risk populations.
2. Collection of health-effects data.
3. Development of dose-response curves.
4. Collection of environmental quality data.
5. Development of exposure profiles.
6. Integration of health and exposure data (steps 3 and 5).

Below we discuss each of these steps in more detail.

Step 1: Identification and Characterization of High Risk Populations

Ambient pollution frequently affects only selected segments of the population. For example, the elderly, asthmatics, and individuals suffering from other respiratory diseases are those most sensitive to suspended particulates. Other

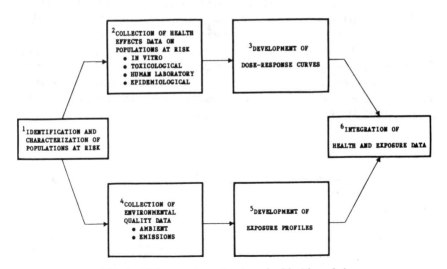

FIG. 1—*Major steps in performing a health risk analysis.*

segments of the high-risk population are those with exceptionally high exposure such as smokers or those with occupational exposure such as miners or asbestos workers. A key task in developing health-based standards consists of identifying and characterizing sensitive populations at risk to the pollutants of concern. Demographic information on these individuals can be obtained from sources such as the Bureau of Census and the National Center for Health Statistics. Table 1 gives demographics on populations at risk from ambient exposures to particulate matter.

Step 2: Collection of Health Effects Data

Health data can be obtained from four different types of studies: in vitro, animal toxicological, human laboratory, and epidemiological.[4]

In vitro studies are tests of chemicals for mutagenicity in bacteria or for transforming action on cell cultures from higher organisms. Their main use is as a relatively quick initial screening of potential carcinogens. Mutagenic chemicals may then be screened in animal studies for carcinogenicity.

Animal toxicological and human laboratory studies are laboratory experiments in which the responses from subjects exposed to the chemical are compared with those of control subjects. Epidemiological data are real world field data which may be either longitudinal (data on health effects for specific individuals or communities over time) or cross sectional (data on health effects for different communities at one point in time) or a combination of both. Epidemiological data are further categorized as retrospective or prospective. Retrospective or case-control studies involve first matching cases (persons suffering a specific health problem, for example, pancreatic cancer) with controls (persons free of the problem) on the basis of sex, age, race, and other potential confounding factors and then investigating whether the cases have a history of greater exposure to the chemical in question than do the controls. Prospective studies start with persons at the same point in time who show none of the specific health effects under investigation, record their characteristics, and then track their future exposures and the future occurrence of specific health effects. Epidemiological studies are the most desirable basis for developing health based air and water standards because they are real world data.

Step 3: Development of Dose-Response Curves

The preponderance of health data is for observable effects at high doses. In the real world, however, health effects might result from exposures to low levels of pollution. Hence, a critical step in analyzing health effects data is to

---

[4]Human laboratory studies are often incorrectly called human clinical studies in air pollution literature. This is a misnomer whose use should be discouraged. Clinical studies involve the random assignment of disease patients to one treatment or another and are used to assess the value of different treatments, not the effect of different insults.

TABLE 1—High risk population subgroups for exposure to airborne particulate matter.

Subgroup	Population Estimates	Rationale (or Criteria)	Observational/Associations Supporting Increased Sensitivity
Individuals with chronic obstructive pulmonary diseases Bronchitis Bronchiectasis Emphysema	7 800 000 [1]	mucus hypersecretion and blocked airways may predispose individuals to bronchospasm; enlarged airspaces increase blood flow resistance through the pulmonary capillary network, increasing cardiac stress	many of the deaths and illnesses during and after air pollution episodes were among people with pre-existing obstructive diseases [2-5]
Individuals with cardiovascular disease	16 100 000 [6]	enhanced sensitivity to difficulties in breathing	many deaths and hospitalizations during pollution episodes among cardiovascular patients (Martin, 1964) [2,3]
Individuals with influenza	unknown	increased sensitivity of respiratory epithelium [7]	influenza patients were more sensitive to $NaNO_3$ during their period of sickness [7] highest mortality during influenza epidemic on days with highest PM [5]
Asthmatics	6 000 000 [1]	hyperreactive airways [8]	sulfuric acid enhanced response to bronchoconstrictive agent in asthmatics, not in normals (Utell et al., 1981)
Elderly	24 658 000 >65 years old [6]	reduced lung elasticity immunologically deficient	many of the deaths and illnesses during air pollution episodes were among elderly [2,5,10]
Children	46 300 000 >14 years old [6]	immunological immaturity implies diminished protection [11] childhood respiratory infection might prevent the lungs from reaching their full size at maturity [12,13] children likely to spend a greater amount of time outdoors and to be more active; probably higher ventilation rates and thus, increased inhalation of pollutants	increased acute respiratory disease with high particles, SO_x [14,15] effects of acute respiratory disease acquired during childhood persisted until adolescence or young adulthood [16,17]
Smokers	50 000 000 [18]	urban lung cancer in smokers greater [19] combinations of PM and carcinogens may enhance response increased tracheobronchial deposition [20]	frequency of respiratory symptoms and diseases greater in smokers exposed to same occupational or community pollution as nonsmokers [21,22]
Mouth or oronasal breathers	15% of population [23,24]	increased particle penetration	

extrapolate effects at low dose levels from effects at high dose levels. Different mathematical models can be used to accomplish this. Five such models used in cancer assessment that have received much attention in the open scientific literature are: probit, logit, one-hit, multi-hit, and multi-stage. Each of these models is based on different mathematical formulae and biological assumptions. Table 2 gives the mathematical formulation of each of these models. For a discussion of the multi-hit model, see Van Ryzin; for the multi-stage see Ref *25* and for a comparison between models, see Refs *26–28*. For a general discussion of theoretical basis of these and other models, see Refs *29, 30*.

Step 4: Collection of Environmental Quality Data

Ambient pollution conditions can be either measured directly or can be estimated from emissions data using diffusion models. Tables 3 and 4 list some major air and water quality data bases; and Table 5 gives models for projecting ambient levels from emissions. Table 6 lists other ambient air and water models.

TABLE 2—*Mathematical dose-response models.*

Ranges of Model	$P(d)$	Parameters
Probit	$\Phi(a + Bd_{(\lambda)})$	$-\infty < a < \infty$
	where $\Phi(t) = (2\pi)^{-1/2} \displaystyle\int_{-\infty}^{t} e^{-u^2/2} du$	$0 \le B$
	and $d_{(\lambda)} = \begin{cases} \lambda^{-1}(d^\lambda - 1) & \text{if } \lambda > 0 \\ \log d & \text{if } \lambda = 0 \end{cases}$	$0 \le \lambda$
Logit	$F(a + Bd_{(\lambda)})$	$-\infty < a < \infty$
		$0 \le B$
	where $F(t) = \exp(t)/(1 + \exp t)$	$0 \le \lambda$
One-hit	$1 - \exp(-a - Bd)$	$a \ge 0$
		$B \ge 0$
Multi-hit	$G(a + Bd)$	$a \ge 0$
		$B \ge 0$
	where $G(t) = \displaystyle\int_{0}^{t} u^{k-1} e^{-u} du/\Gamma(k)$	$K > 0$
	and $\Gamma(k) = \displaystyle\int_{0}^{\infty} u^{k-1} e^{-u} du$	
Multi-stage	$1 - \exp\left(-\displaystyle\sum_{i=0}^{K} a_i d^i\right)$	$K > 0$, integer $a_i \ge 0$

TABLE 3—*Major emissions databases* [31].

Name	Pollutants	Year (2)	Coverage	Comments
National Emissions Data System (NEDS)	TSP, SOX, NOX, HC, CO	1973–1979	U.S.	
Sulfate Regional Experiment (SURE)	TSP, SO_2, SO_4, NOX	1977–1978	Eastern U.S., part of Canada	has detailed short-time estimates
Multistate Atmospheric Power Production Study (MAP35)	TSP, SO_2, SO_4, HC, CO	1978	U.S., part of Canada	based on NEDS, SURE
Unified Inventory	SOX	1980	U.S., Canada	utility industry in more detail
Hazardous and Trace Emissions System (HATREMS)	Pollutants not regulated by primary ambient air standard		U.S.	
Emissions History Information System (EHIS)	NA^a		NA	EPA data base containing reports of U.S. pollutant emissions estimates for previous years
Aerometric and Emissions Reporting Systems (AEROS)	NA		NA	EPA data base on water quality
National Pollutant Discharge Elimination System (NPDES)	11 water pollutants	1974–1981	Federal Region 5	covers industrial and municipal point sources
Environmental Data Analysis System (EDAS)	5 particles liquid effluents solid waste gaseous emissions			

^{a}NA = not available.

TABLE 4—*Major air and water quality data bases.*

Name	Pollutants	Year(s)	Coverage
Storage and Retrieval of Aerometric Data System (SAROAD)	all monitored pollutants	1973–1983	U.S.
Storage and Retrieval for Water Quality Data (STORET)	all monitored pollutants	1970–1983	U.S.
Distribution Register of Organic Pollutants in Water (WATERDROP)	organics	NA	U.S.
Environmental Contaminant Monitoring Program	20 pesticides organics heavy metals	NA	U.S.
Pesticides Soils Monitoring Program	pesticides	NA	U.S.

TABLE 5—*Selected ambient models.*

Name	Approximate Geographic Range	Time Intervals	Comments
CRSTER (EPA)	few kilometers	hourly to annual	single source
CDM (EPA)	0 to 30 km	annual	multiple source
RAM (EPA)	0 to 30 km	hourly to 24 hour	multiple source
MESOPUFF (EPA)	30 to 200 km	up to a few days	multiple source
PRAHM (?)	30 to 200 km	up to a few days	multiple source
ASTRAP (Argonne National Laboratory)	200 to 2000 km	seasonal to annual	multiple source
RCDM (EPA)	200 to 2000 km	seasonal to annual	multiple source
OME (Canadian)	200 to 2000 km	seasonal to annual	multiple source

Step 5: Development of Exposure Profiles

Factors that must be considered in estimating exposures to air pollution differ from those that must be considered in estimating exposures to water pollution. Three factors that must be taken into account in developing air exposure profiles are:

(*a*) Pollution levels differ considerably from one environment to another.

(*b*) Individuals spend time in many different environments.

(*c*) Models are needed for integrating exposure data with time budget data.

Several models have been proposed for integrating time budget data with exposure data. Perhaps the most popular of these is the National Ambient Air Quality Exposure Model (NEM) program prepared for U.S. Environmental Protection Agency (EPA) by PEDCO Environmental, Inc.

The output of this program is a table showing for each level of a specified pol-

TABLE 6—*Other ambient air and water models* [31].

Model Acronym	Name of Model
	WATER QUALITY MODELS
SEM	Simplified Estuary Model
ES001	Estuarine Water Quality Model
DEM	Dynamic Estuary Model
TTM	Tidal Temperature Model
HAR03	Water Quality Model
FEDBAKO3	Water Quality Feedback Model
PLUME	Outfall Plume Model
QUAL-II	Stream Quality Model
REDEQL.EPA	Computer Program for Chemical Equilibria in Aqueous Systems
RECEIV-II	Receiving Water Model
EXPLORE-I	Water Quality Model
MS. CLEANER	Multi-Segment Comprehensive Lake Ecosystem Analyzer for Environmental Resources
DIURNAL	Receiving Water Model
	WATER RUNOFF MODELS
AGRUN	Agricultural Watershed Runoff Model
ARM II	Agricultural Runoff Model (Version II)
GWMTM1	One Dimensional Groundwater Mass Transport Model
GWMTM2	Two Dimensional Groundwater Mass Transport Model
EPAURA	Non-Point Runoff Model for a Single Storm Even in an Urban/Suburban Setting
EPARRB	Non-Point Runoff Model for a Rural Setting
NPS	Non-Point Source Pollutant Loading Model
	AIR QUALITY MODELS
HIWAY 2	EPA HIWAY Model
APRAC-1A	Air Pollution Research Advisory Committee Model 1A
APRAC-2	Air Pollution Research Advisory Committee Model 2
PSM'S	Point Source Models
TEM	Texas Episodic Model
TCM	Texas Climatological Model
LIRAQ	Livermore Regional Air Quality Model
PAL	Point, Area, Line Source Algorithm
CRSTER	Single Source Model
AQDM	Air Quality Display Model
RAM	Gaussian Plume Multiple Source Air Quality Algorithm
VALLEY	Gaussian Plume Dispersion Algorithm
...	Nonlinear Rollback/Rollforward Model
SAI	Systems Applications, Inc., Model
CDM/CDMQC	Climatological Display Model
REPS	Regional Emissions Projection System
ISC	Industrial Source Complex Model
	ECONOMIC MODELS
SEAS	Strategic Environmental Assessment System
COPMOD1	U.S. Copper Industry Model
CONMOD	Construction Model
PTM	Steel Industry Model
CARMOD	Automobile Demand Model
ABTRES	Abatement and Residual Forecasting Model
	OTHER MODELS
WRAP	Waste Resources Allocation Program
MMMSPT-EPM	Mathematical Model for Fast Screening Procedure for Testing the Effects of Pollutants in Mammals
NRM	Nonionizing Radiation Models

lutant, the number of person-hours of exposure to that level. A separate table is produced for each of 12 age-occupation groups.

Another program is the Simulation of Human Air Pollution Exposure (SHAPE) model. Greater computer cost makes this program less widely used than NEM. Outputs of this model are in the form of a 3-dimensional histogram with the axes being pollution concentration levels, time spent in different environments, and percent of population exposed (Fig. 2).

Factors that must be taken into account in developing water exposure profiles are:

(a) pollution levels in drinking water and ground water;
(b) pollution levels in waterways from which seafood is obtained;
(c) bioconcentration factor of chemicals in seafood; and
(d) amount of fish consumed.

A discussion of these factors is given in a Federal Register Notice of March 1979.

Step 6: Integration of Health and Exposure Data

The findings from risk assessments are in the form of X persons at risk to health effect Y as a result of Z exposure. An example of such a computation is given in the discussion of Water Quality Criteria.

Difficulties with Risk Assessment

Each of the steps discussed above presents difficulties. Some of these are:

Step 1—For many of the chemicals considered for regulation the demographic data needed for identification of a high-risk population do not exist.

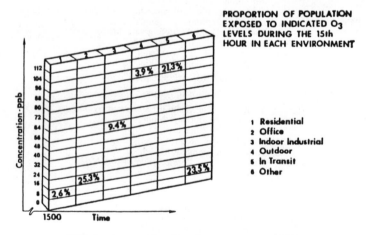

FIG. 2—*An example of hourly ozone exposures* [32].

Step 2—Animal, human laboratory, and epidemiological data all have disadvantages as well as advantages. Animal and human laboratory studies are carried out under laboratory conditions and allow designs which can investigate interactions with specific confounding factors and which can, in the case of human laboratory studies, allow focusing on well characterized subpopulations. For animal studies, detailed histological follow-up is possible.

Several major short-comings of animal toxicological studies include the following issues. First, there is currently no validated model for quantitatively converting animal data to human data. This is because little is known quantitatively about differences between animals and humans with respect to factors such as absorption, metabolism, disposition, and excretion. At present U.S. EPA relies on the following equation for carcinogens to relate animal data to humans

$$\frac{d_H}{d_A} = \left(\frac{W_A}{W_H}\right)^{1/3}$$

where

d_H = human dose in mg of chemical per kg of body weight,
W_H = human body weight in kg; and
d_A, W_A = same quantities for animals.

This equation is based on the assumption that equally effective dose levels of direct-acting drugs are proportional to body surface area. This is justified both by theory and by some drug activity data. Other formulae, however have been proposed and need to be carefully examined in terms of applicability to chemicals in general, including non-carcinogenic toxicants.

A second major problem is the question as to whether the chemical under study or its metabolites is the direct toxicant and whether the metabolic path of the chemical is the same in humans and animals.

A third consideration difficult to quantify is the difference between inbred homogeneous animal strains and the heterogeneous general human population.

Major shortcomings of human laboratory studies begin with the lack of realism of the laboratory setting. Exposure levels, air mixtures, psychological stresses, and behavior patterns are different in the laboratory and the real world. Second, for ethical reasons, only relatively minor effects—such as temporary reduction in airway resistance—can be studied and only minimal histological follow-up can be done. Third, laboratory subjects are often exposed to the chemical via a different route than that most common in real life settings, a fact which leads to problems in dose-response estimation.

Fourth, human laboratory studies rarely involve more than 20 subject and often fewer because of the expense and difficulty of such studies. To a lesser extent this small sample size problem may also afflict animal studies, particularly those performed on larger species.

Epidemiological data frequently suffer from such problems as the following. First, the exposure burden on individuals is often inadequately measured, for example, by using data from stationary outdoor monitoring stations to assess the exposure of individuals living in the vicinity. Second, techniques of pollution measurement, definitions of health endpoints and standards of reporting of data on health endpoints, particularly non-fatal endpoints, may vary from area to area or within one area over time. Third, confounding factors such as smoking habits and socioeconomic status may not be adequately recorded or may be highly associated with exposure, making distinction between the effects of each impossible. Fourth, while associations between exposure and response in carefully designed and controlled randomized experiments are evidence of causal relationships, such associations in epidemiologic data may be the result of an association of both exposure and response with an overlooked third factor.

Additional problems specific to retrospective studies are inability to determine past exposure levels due to poor recall by the subjects and biased selection of the controls, who, for convenience, are often taken as all patients in a hospital not suffering from the specific health effects under study. Berkson has demonstrated how the latter technique can lead to spurious association, a phenomenon known as Berkson's fallacy [33, 34].

Additional problems specific to prospective studies are the expense and trouble required to follow subjects over long periods and the possibility that withdrawal from the study may be associated with either exposure or the specific health effects in question.

Step 3—One of the major problems with modeling dose-response relationships is that different models frequently will give sharply different results, and it may be difficult to determine which model is appropriate. Sometimes a goodness of fit test with the available data may reject a model, as is the case with the one-hit model in example 1 below, but often several models fit the current data well but give quite different extrapolations. Theoretical mechanisms have been proposed for some health effects, such as initiation and promotion stages in chemical carcinogenesis or multi-hit theories for radiation carcinogenesis. However, mechanisms for most forms of toxic action are as yet poorly verified or non-existent.

To illustrate this problem, Table 7 lists published thyroid carcinoma data on ethylene thiourea (ETU) at high doses as well as predicted values from the probit, logit, one-hit, multi-hit, and multi-stage models for these data. Either direct inspection or computation of chi-square statistics rules out the one-hit model as unacceptable but the other four fit acceptably. Table 8 gives safe level doses at the 10^{-5} (an excess risk of one out of 100 thousand people), 10^{-6}, and 10^{-7} risk levels for the five models. Table 8 shows that these models yield different results when extrapolated to low doses. At the 10^{-5} risk level, for example, the predicted dose based on the probit model is 6.1×10^{-3} as compared to 9.6 for the multi-stage and 45 for the multi-hit model. In this case, therefore, the multi-hit model yields doses that are about five times

TABLE 7—*Goodness of fit of competing models.*

Substance: Ethylene thiourea (ETU)
Animal tested: Rat
Response: Thyroid carcinoma

Dose (ppm)	0	5	25	125	250
Number tested	72	75	73	73	69
Observed number of responses	2	2	1	2	16
EXPECTED NUMBER OF RESPONSES					
Probit	1	1	2	5	15
Logit	1	1	1	4	15
One-hit	1	2	4	16	26
Multi-hit	2	2	2	2	16
Multi-stage	1	2	2	3	15

TABLE 8—*Virtually safe dose (VSD) levels for different levels of excess risk.*

Substance: Ethylene thiourea (ETU)
Animal tested: Rat
Response: Thyroid carcinoma

Excess Risk	Probit	Logit	One-Hit	Multi-Hit	Multi-Stage
10^{-2}	5.2×10	6.1×10	5.4	1.3×10	9.4×10
10^{-3}	9.5	1.1×10	0.5	8.9×10	4.4×10
10^{-4}	1.5	1.8	5.4×10^{-2}	6.3×10	2.1×10
10^{-5}	2.4×10^{-1}	2.9×10^{-1}	5.4×10^{-3}	4.5×10	9.9
10^{-6}	3.8×10^{-2}	4.7×10^{-2}	5.4×10^{-4}	3.3×10	4.5
10^{-7}	6.1×10^{-3}	7.4×10^{-3}	5.4×10^{-5}	4.4	2.1

greater than the multi-stage model and nearly a thousand times greater than the probit or logit models.

As a second example, consider Table 9 which lists liver hepatoma data for female mice exposed to DDT. Here all 5 models show adequate fit as judged by chi-square tests or by direct inspection. However, looking at Table 10 we see that the multi-hit model gives a VSD about 100 times larger than a multi-stage model and 10^8 times larger than a probit model.

In addition, the proper transformation of dose for the probit and logit models must be determined. The most common choices are the Box-Cox transformation

$$d_{(\lambda)} = \begin{cases} (d^{\lambda} - 1)/\lambda & \text{if } \lambda > 0 \\ \log d & \text{if } \lambda = 0 \end{cases}$$

with λ to be estimated and the threshold model

$$d^* = \begin{cases} d - t & \text{if } d > t \\ 0 & \text{if } d \leq t \end{cases}$$

with t to be estimated.

TABLE 9—*Goodness of fit of competing models.*

Substance: Dichlorodiphenyltrichloroethane (DDT)
Animal tested: CF-1 female mice
Response: Liver hepatoma

Dose (ppm)	0	2	10	50	250
Number tested	111	105	124	104	90
Observed number of responses	4	4	11	13	60
EXPECTED NUMBER OF RESPONSES					
Probit	3	5	9	19	58
Logit	4	5	9	17	59
One-hit	4	4	9	21	56
Multi-hit	6	5	7	15	60
Multi-stage	5	5	8	14	60

TABLE 10—*Virtually safe dose (VSD) levels for different levels of excess risk.*

Substance: Dichlorodiphenyltrichloroethane (DDT)
Animal tested: CF-1 female mice
Response: Liver hepatoma

Excess Risk	Probit	Logit	One-Hit	Multi-Hit	Multi-Stage
10^{-2}	0.94	1.2	2.7	11.8	4.9
10^{-3}	1.2×10^{-2}	1.6×10^{-2}	2.7×10^{-1}	2.9	4.9×10^{-1}
10^{-4}	1.2×10^{-4}	1.6×10^{-4}	2.7×10^{-2}	7.4×10^{-1}	4.9×10^{-2}
10^{-5}	1.2×10^{-6}	1.6×10^{-6}	2.7×10^{-3}	1.9×10^{-1}	4.9×10^{-3}
10^{-6}	1.2×10^{-8}	1.6×10^{-8}	2.7×10^{-4}	4.8×10^{-2}	4.9×10^{-4}
10^{-7}	1.2×10^{-10}	1.6×10^{-10}	2.7×10^{-5}	1.2×10^{-2}	4.9×10^{-5}

On theoretical grounds, thresholds are ruled out for agents with a genotoxic effect but may occur for agents with an epigenetic effect. (The ED01 study showed an apparent threshold for bladder cancers caused by 2 acetylamino-fluorene but a Box-Cox transformation without threshold fit the data better [35]. A further argument against threshold models is that even for substances with individual thresholds, the individual thresholds vary so that no meaningful population threshold can be identified.

A further problem, mentioned earlier, is the difficulty of converting a dose-response curve estimated for animal experiments to one for humans or a curve estimated for one exposure route to that for another route. No conversion method currently has much empirical support, for either species or route conversion.

Another problem that arises in dose-response curve fitting is deciding whether any curve should be fit in the absence of statistically significant differences between treated and control groups. As an example, consider U.S. EPA's water quality criterion for beryllium. The EPA's analysis was based on the following data from Ref *36*.

(*a*) 4 tumors in 26 control animals, and

(*b*) 8 tumors in 33 animals at dose 5 ppm.

A chi-square statistic for a difference in tumorigenicity rates has value 0.26 on one degree of freedom, not close to significant. Inserting the observed rates of 0.153846 and 0.242424 into any of the one-hit, multi-hit, or multi-stage models,[5] we get 0.534 ppb as the maximum likelihood estimate of virtually safe dose (VSD) for an excess risk of 10^{-5}. Yet it seems questionable whether data which show no greater difference in rates than can occur by chance are adequate to justify such standards.

Step 4—The major problem in this step is the unevenness of data collection in different cities and among pollutants within a single city.

Step 5—The problem of uneven or unreliable data is considerable in this step. The infiltration of airborne pollutants to the indoors varies greatly from one structure to another. The NEM computer model uses estimates of infiltration based on small, nonrandom samples of buildings so the reliability of these estimates is unclear.

Also, the NEM program uses survey data to estimate the proportion of time individuals spend in various activities. There is considerable variability in these data, introduced by (1) inability of individual respondents to recall their weekly activity patterns accurately, and (2) inherent variability in these patterns between individuals or over time for a single individual. Yet for reasons of cost, the NEM assumes only three possible activity patterns for each age-occupation group. Similar problems obtain in survey data regarding amount of swimming or fish consumption when one is concerned with exposure to water pollution.

A third problem that arises with indoor air pollutants is that devices, such as gas stoves, which produce indoor air pollutants often operate intermittently. This makes it necessary to estimate transient as well as steady-state concentrations of pollutants.

When radioactive substances are being considered, an additional task that is needed at this step, is to keep track of the evolution of daughter isotopes over time.

Step 6—In real life, one expects the possibility of multiple exposures to the same substance by different routes and to different substances with possibly synergistic or antagonistic effects. The number of combinations of substances is too vast to permit laboratory studies of more than a handful of such possible interactions. Consequently, considerable uncertainty must exist about the cumulative health effects of a combination of exposures to specified levels of different substances even when individual dose-response curves are known.

At each steps 1 through 5 there is uncertainty about actual figures and consequently confidence limits may be obtained as well as point estimates. One

---

[5] If the data consist only of two data points, the one-hit, multi-hit, and multi-stage models yield the same results.

thus obtains at step 6 upper and lower confidence limits on, as well as a best estimate of, the number of health effects expected from a specified emission of pollutant and on the virtually safe level, the level at which risk is below the tolerable limit. Since lower confidence limits may differ by an order of magnitude or more from best estimates, the choice of which to use for standard setting can be quite consequential. (In Table 11, we illustrate this by comparing the maximum likelihood estimates of VSD with the 95% lower confidence limits for DDT.)

The critical question at the end of a risk analysis is, of course, what is an acceptable risk level. For carcinogens, U.S. EPA has recommended that the level be set at between 1 out of 100 000 people (10^{-5}) and 1 out of 10 000 000 people (10^{-7}) at risk. To our knowledge, however, neither the EPA nor anyone else has suggested what might be an acceptable risk for asthma attacks, colds, intestinal diseases, nervous disorders, and other illnesses possibly related to environmental pollution. Finally, to place the findings from environmental risk assessment into perspective, it is important to compare environmental risks with risks of other events such as crossing the street and occupational hazards.

These last two questions, however, are properly considered as part of risk management, not risk analysis. Since they involve clearly political or philosophical questions, this phase of the process should be kept separate from the purely scientific process of risk assessment.

Current Use of Risk Assessment

Table 12 outlines the degree to which risk assessment is being used to develop some of the major environmental health-based standards. A more detailed discussion of the table follows.

National Ambient Air Quality Standards (NAAQS)

At present little consideration is being given to risk analysis in developing NAAQS. The current process for developing NAAQS consists of assessing

TABLE 11—*Confidence limits of excess risks at the 10^{-5} excess risk level.*

Substance: Dichlorodiphenyltrichloroethane (DDT)
Animal tested: CF-1 female mice
Response: Liver hepatoma

Lower Confidence	Probit	Logit	One-Hit	Multi-Hit	Multi-Stage
Virtually safe dose	1.20×10^{-6}	1.60×10^{-6}	2.7×10^{-3}	1.9×10^{-1}	4.9×10^{-3}
90.0%	1.02×10^{-6}	1.31×10^{-6}	2.2×10^{-3}	2.1×10^{-2}	3.0×10^{-3}
95.0%	0.99×10^{-6}	1.27×10^{-6}	2.1×10^{-3}	1.2×10^{-2}	2.7×10^{-3}
97.5%	0.96×10^{-6}	1.23×10^{-6}	2.0×10^{-3}	6.8×10^{-3}	2.5×10^{-3}
99.0%	0.93×10^{-6}	1.19×10^{-6}	1.9×10^{-3}	3.6×10^{-3}	2.3×10^{-3}

TABLE 12—*Use of risk assessment variables in developing selected environmental health based regulations.*

Regulations	High-Risk Populations	Health Effects Data	Dose-Response Curves	Environmental Quality Data	Integration of Health and Exposure Data
1. National Ambient Air Quality Standards (Sections 108 & 109 of the Clean Air Act)	developing models	yes	developing models	developing models	developing models
2. National Emission Standards for Hazardous Air Pollutants Section 112 of the Clean Air Act)	unknown	yes	probably	unknown	unknown
3. Water Quality Criteria (Section 304 of the Clean Water Act)	no	yes	yes	partially	partially
4. Toxic Substance Control Act	no	yes	yes	yes	yes
5. Resource Conservation and Recovery Act	no	yes	probably	unknown	unknown
6. Occupational Safety and Health Act	no	yes	yes	partially	yes
7. Federal Insecticide, Fungicide and Rodenticide Act. Federal Environmental Pesticide Control Act	yes	yes	yes		
8. Federal Food, Drug and Cosmetic Act	no	yes	none for carcinogens in food; some for cosmetics	no	no
9. Consumer Product Safety Act	no	yes	no	no	no
10. National Environmental Policy Act (Radiation)	no	yes	yes	yes	yes
11. USDA	no	yes	yes	yes	yes

critical health effects studies and setting standards at levels which provide an adequate margin of safety for even the most sensitive members of the population. Little consideration has been given in the standard-setting process to factors such as the size of the sensitive population and their exposures from all sources. The Agency, however, is funding research in the area. The NAAQS Exposure Models (NEM) developed in 1981–1982 for carbon monoxide, nitrogen oxides, and particulates are an attempt to include these factors in the risk assessment process [*37,38,39*].

National Emission Standards for Hazardous Air Pollutants (NESHAPS)

It is difficult to determine to what extent risk assessment is being utilized to develop NESHAPS because the last NESHAP regulation was promulgated in 1976 (vinyl chloride). However, indications exist that EPA is currently revising the air carcinogen policy which was developed by the previous administration. This policy contained a risk assessment approach to regulating carcinogens.

Water Quality Criteria

To a greater extent than in any other regulations, the U.S. EPA is using risk analysis to develop water quality criteria. In general the criteria are expressed in terms of the risks (10^{-5}, 10^{-6}, 10^{-7}) associated with various concentrations of pollutants in water. Variables considered in the EPA analyses include the bioconcentration of the chemical in fish, the amount of fish eaten, and the weight of experimental individuals. In many respects, however, the EPA analyses are limited by poor quality data, the failure to take into account factors such as the size of the sensitive population, and reliance on unvalidated extrapolation models. As a result, EPA's criteria are frequently unrealistic. EPA's health-based criterion for arsenic [40], for example, is based on a dose-response model which indicates that of the 210 million people currently living in the U.S., 19 to 95 million will incur arsenic-induced skin cancer. This is based on assuming a Weibull distribution for arsenic induced skin cancer with $1 - \exp(-BXt^v)$ being the probability of contracting skin cancer after being exposed for time t to arsenic at dose X in grams/liter. From this one derives $BXt_m^v/(\ln 2 + BXt_m^v)$ as the median probability of ever contracting skin cancer, given lifelong exposure to dose X; t_m being the median lifetime in the population in question. B and V are estimated to be 2.41×10^{-8}, and 3.853, respectively, while t_m is 68 years. X is taken to be between 245 μg/L and 2100 μg/L [41].

The conclusions seem ludicrous given that the National Cancer Institute reports only 17 400 skin cancer cases in 1982. Over a median lifetime of 68 years, this is only 1.18 million cases from all causes.

Toxic Substance Control Act (TSCA) and Resource Conservation and Recovery Act (RCRA)

As with NESHAPS there have not been any TSCA or RCRA regulations to determine whether the Agency has taken into account all the necessary risk information in developing standards. Of particular importance in this regard will be the Agency's regulation of PCBs in the utility industry.

Federal Insecticide, Fungicide and Rodenticide Act (FIFRA)

The Environmental Fate Branch of the Hazard Evaluation Division, Office of Pesticides, and Toxic Substances assesses exposure to pesticides of:

(a) general population,
(b) agricultural applicators,

(c) fieldworkers,
(d) industrial users, and
(e) home users,

in order to prepare risk assessments both for single-dose effects like neurotoxicity and for chronic effects like cancer.

Consumer Product Safety Commission (CPSC)

CPSC has used exposure assessment modeling in establishing regulations for benzidine-based dyes, formaldehyde, and indoor air pollutants. Health effects were summarily discussed in promulgating these regulations, but dose-response curves were not estimated, and risk assessment as we have outlined it was not used.

Department of Agriculture (USDA)

USDA has recently combined data on national bacon consumption, analytical chemistry methods, and carcogenicity response data to estimate the increase in human cancer due to nitrosamines in bacon.

Office of Radiation Programs, (USEPA)

Under the National Environmental Policy Act of 1969 and the Clean Air Act amendments of 1977, EPA is responsible for regulating radioactive pollutants. Models are used to estimate radionuclide concentrations in air, ground, water, and food; to estimate doses to 11 human organs in rem/year; and, finally, to estimate the number of health effects/year in the population.

Legislative Activities

As evidenced by several bills that are currently before Congress, the federal government is increasingly relying on risk assessment. Some of these bills are:

1. Risk Analysis Research and Demonstration Act of 1981—a bill to establish a coordinated program to improve and facilitate the use of risk analyses in decisions related to human life, health, and protection of the environment;

2. Clean Air Act Amendments of 1981—a bill to amend the Clean Air Act to maximize protection of public health while minimizing social and economic disruption;

3. Food Additive Safety Amendments of 1981—a bill to amend the Federal Food, Drug, and Cosmetic Act authorizing the regulation of food additives on the basis of risk assessment; and

4. Food Safety Amendments of 1981—a bill to amend several food safety related acts to provide for risk assessment.

In addition, the House Democratic Caucus task force on the environment has drafted a position paper (April 1982) which calls for:

... implementing a research program designed ultimately to tell us quickly the risks of chemicals ... [and] improving our ability as a society to do quantitative risk assessment ... Only by vastly increasing the resources devoted to the development and testing of risk assessment techniques will we be able to regulate in a totally rational fashion ...

References

[1] Education, and Welfare, "Prevalence of Selected Chronic Respiratory Conditions, United States—1970," U.S. Department of Health, Publication No. (HRA) 74-1511, Series 10, Number 84, Rockville, Md., Sept. 1973.

[2] "Mortality and Morbidity During the London Fog of December 1952," Ministry of Health, London, Her Majesty's Stationery Office, 1954.

[3] Martin, A. E., "Mortality and Morbidity Statistics and Air Pollution," Proceedings, Royal Society of Medicine, Vol. 57; 1964, pp. 969-975.

[4] Lawther, P. J., Waller, R. E., and Henderson, M., "Air Pollution and Exacerbations of Bronchitis," Thorax, Vol. 25, 1970, pp. 525-539.

[5] Martin, A. E., and Bradley, W. H., "Mortality, Fog and Atmospheric Pollutin—An Investigation During the Winter of 1958-59," Monthly Bulletin of the Ministry of Health and the Public Health Laboratory Service, Vol. 19, 1960, pp. 56-73.

[6] "Statistical Abstract of the United States 1980," 101st edition, Bureau of the Census, U.S. Department of Commerce, 1980.

[7] Utell, M. J., Aquilina, A. T., Hall, W. J., Speers, D. M., Douglas, R. G., Jr., Gibb, F. R., Morrow, P. E., and Hyde, R. W., "Development of Airway Reactivity to Nitrates in Subjects with Influenza," American Review of Respiratory Diseases, Vol. 121, 1980, pp. 233-241.

[8] Bouhuys, H. A., Holtzman, M. J., Sheller, J. R., and Nadel, J. A., "Bronchial Hyperreactivity," American Review of Respiratory Disease, Vol. 121, 1980, pp. 389-413.

[9] Cotes, J. E., "Lung Function Assessment and Application in Medicine," Blackwell Scientific Publications, London, England, 1979, pp. 266-267.

[10] Greenburg, L., Field, F., Reed, J. I., and Erhardt, C. L., "Air Pollution and Morbidity in New York," Journal of the American Medical Association, Vol. 182, 1962, pp. 161-164.

[11] Eisen, H. N., Immunology, Harper and Row, Hagerstown, Md., 1976, p. 410.

[12] Bouhuys, A., The Physiology of Breathing: A Textbook for Medical Students, Grume and Stratton, New York, 1977.

[13] Speizer, F. E., Ferris, B., Bishop, Y. M. M., and Spengler, J., "Respiratory Disease Rates and Pulmonary Function in Children Associated with NO_2 Exposure," American Review of Respiratory Diseases, Vol. 121, 1980, pp. 3-10.

[14] Lebowitz, M. D., Cassell, E. J., and McCarroll, J. R., "Health and the Urban Environment. XV. Acute Respiratory Episodes as Reactions by Sensitive Individuals to Air Pollution and Weather," Environmental Research, Vol. 5, 1972, pp. 135-141.

[15] Douglas, J. W. B. and Waller, R. E., "Air Pollution and Respiratory Infection in Children," British Journal of Preventive and Social Medicine, Vol. 20, 1966, pp. 1-8.

[16] Colley, J. R. T., Douglas, J. W. B., and Reid, D. D., "Respiratory Disease in Young Adults: Influence of Early Childhood Lower Respiratory Tract Illness, Social Class, Air Pollution, and Smoking," British Medical Journal, Vol. 3, 1973, pp. 195-198.

[17] Kiernan, K. E., Colley, J. R. T., Douglas, J. W. B., and Reid, D. D., "Chronic Cough in Young Adults in Relation to Smoking Habits, Childhood Environment, and Chest Illness," Respiratory, 1976, Vol. 33, pp. 236-244.

[18] "The Smoking Digest," U.S. Department of Health, Education and Welfare, Public

Health Service, National Institutes of Health, National Cancer Institute, Bethesda, Md., 1977, p. 5.

[19] Doll, R., "Atmospheric Pollution and Lung Cancer," *Environmental Health Perspective*, Vol. 22, 1978, pp. 23-31.

[20] Albert, R. E., Lippmann, M., Peterson, H. T., Jr., Berger, J., Sanborn, K., and Bohning, D., "Bronchial Deposition and Clearance of Aerosols," *Archives of Internal Medicine*, Vol. 131, 1973, pp. 115-127.

[21] Lambert, P. M. and Reid, D. D., "Smoking, Air Pollution, and Bronchitis in Britain," *Lancet*, Vol. I, 1970, pp. 853-857.

[22] "Criteria for a Recommended Standard: Occupational Exposure to Cotton Dust," National Institute for Occupational Safety and Health, U.S. Department of Health and Human Services, Washington, D.C., 1976.

[23] Niinimaa, V., Cole, P., Mintz, S., and Shephard, R. J., "Oronasal Distribution of Respiratory Airflow," *Respiratory Physiology*, Vol. 43, 1981, pp. 69-75.

[24] Saibene, F., Morgnoni, P., Lafortuna, C. L., and Mostardi, R., "Oronasal Breathing Duration Exercise," *Pfuegers Archiology*, Vol. 378, 1978, pp. 65-69.

[25] Crump, K. S., Hoel, D. G., Langley, C. H., Peto, R., "Fundamental Carcinogenic Processes and Their Implications for Low Dose Risk Assessment," *Cancer Research*, Vol. 36, 1976, pp. 2973-2979.

[26] Van Ryzin, J., "Quantitative Risk Assessment," *Journal of Occupational Medicine*, Vol. 22, No. 5, 1980, pp. 321-326.

[27] Van Ryzin, J. and Rai, K., "The Use of Quantal Response Data to Make Predictions," *Scientific Basis of Toxicity Assessment*, H. Witschi, Ed. Biomedical Press, Amsterdam, 1979.

[28] Hoel, D. G., Gaylor, D. W., Kirschstein, R. L., Saffiotti, U., Schneiderman, M. A., "Estimation of Risks of Irreversible, Delayed Toxicity," *Journal of Toxicology and Environmental Health*, Vol. 1, 1975, pp. 133-151.

[29] Arley, N. and Eker, R., "Mechanisms of Carcinogenesis," *Advances in Biological and Medical Physical*, Vol. 8, 1962, p. 375.

[30] Arley, N. "Applications of Stochastic Models for the Analysis of the Mechanisms of Carcinogenesis," *Stochastic Models in Medicine and Biology*, John Gurland, Ed., University of Wisconsin Press, Madison, 1964.

[31] *Handbook for Performing Exposure Assessments*, Exposure Assessment Group Office of Health and Environmental Assessment of U.S. Environmental Protection Agency, Undated.

[32] Moschandreas, D. J., "Exposure to Pollutants and Daily Time Budgets," *Bulletin of the New York Academy of Medicine*, March 1982.

[33] Berkson, J., "The Statistical Study of Association Between Smoking and Lung Cancer," *Mayo Clinic Proceedings*, Vol. 30, 1955, p. 319.

[34] Berkson, J., "Limitations of the Application of Fourfold Table Analysis to Hospital Data," *Biometrics* Vol. 2, 1946, p. 47.

[35] Stallones, R., Corn, M., Crump, K., Davies, J. C., Dole, V., Greenwood, T., Merrill, R., Mirer, F., North, D. W., Omenn, G., Rodricks, J., Slovic, P., Utidjian, H., and Weisburger, E., "Risk Assessment in the Federal Government: Managing the Process," *National Academy Press*, Washington, D.C., 1983.

[36] Schroeder, H. A. and Mitchener, M., "Toxic Effects of Trace Elements on the Reproduction of Mice and Rats," *Archives of Environmental Health*, Vol. 23, 1971, pp. 102-106.

[37] Paul, R., *User's Guide for NAAQS Exposure Model*, U.S. Environmental Protection Agency, 1981.

[38] Johnson, T. and Paul, R., *The NAAQS Exposure Model and Its Application to Nitrogen Dioxide*, U.S. Environmental Protection Agency, 1981.

[39] Johnson, T. and Paul, R. *The NAAQS Exposure Model Applied to Carbon Monoxide*, U.S. Environmental Protection Agency, 1982.

[40] Ambient Water Quality Criteria for Arsenic, 45 FR 79351, U.S. Environment Protection Agency, (1980).

[41] "Trace Elements in Human Nutrition," Technical Report Series No. 532, World Health Organization, 1973.

John K. Taylor[1]

Essential Features of a Laboratory Quality Assurance Program

REFERENCE: Taylor, J. K., "Essential Features of a Laboratory Quality Assurance Program," *Statistics in the Environmental Sciences, ASTM STP 845,* S. M. Gertz and M. D. London, Eds., American Society for Testing and Materials, 1984, pp. 66–73.

ABSTRACT: Progress in the environmental sciences is vitally dependent on reliable data resulting from complex measurement processes. Because of this complexity, the measurement process must be well designed and operate in a state of statistical control. A quality assurance program, including quality control and quality assessment procedures, denotes those features that lead to the production of data under these conditions. The rudimentary features are described together with the expected benefits. Parallelisms are drawn with a well designed manufacturing process.

KEY WORDS: chemical analysis, data quality, good laboratory practices, laboratory accreditation, measurement assurance, quality assessment, quality assurance, quality control, reference materials

The demand for measurement data is ever increasing. Decisions need to be made on such questions as the properties of materials, the quality of the environment, and the health of individuals. Much of the data required must be obtained by sophisticated measurements at levels of sensitivity and accuracy not attainable only a short while ago. Moreover, measurements made by several analysts or laboratories or both often need to be interrelated for use in a decision process. Monitoring programs of regional, national, and even global extent may be involved. The experience of metrologists has demonstrated that data reliability and compatibility are best achieved by a well designed quality assurance program. The basic aspects of such a program are described in the present paper.

Definition of Quality Assurance

Every experimenter knows that the absolute accuracy of any measurement cannot be guaranteed. Yet data are for use, so it must be trustworthy. Its quality

---

[1]Coordinator for Quality Assurance, Center for Analytical Chemistry, National Bureau of Standards, Gaithersburg, Md. 20899.

must be defined, which means that the limits of confidence must be evaluated and stated. The objective of a quality assurance program is to provide a statistical basis for the assignment of such limits.

Quality assurance consists in the establishment of techniques to control quality—quality control—and techniques to evaluate their effectiveness—quality assessment [1]. The measurement process may be developed and implemented so that it has the essential characteristic of a production process, namely, the ability to produce objects—in this case data—with a high degree of reproducibility. Once this is established, the precision is defined and any biases can be usually identified and essentially eliminated or adequately compensated so that requisite data quality is achieved.

The quality assurance procedure followed in a typical production process is illustrated in Fig. 1. Experience dictates the kind and degree of control that must be achieved and maintained to obtain products of desired quality. Random samples are tested or inspected with respect to specifications, to release or accept the production lot, to reject it, or to take corrective actions in the process.

The quality assurance aspects of a typical measurement process are illustrated in Fig. 2. Quality control procedures are used to tune the system to a state of statistical control in which it may be considered as capable of generating an infinite number of measurements of which the data of the moment are a representative sample. Quality assessment procedures are then used to evaluate the quality of the data that are produced. Unfortunately, it is generally impossible intrinsically to fully evaluate the quality of the data on the unknown test materials. However, if the measurement system is in a state of statistical control, known test samples such as reference materials (RM) may be measured concurrently and the results compared with the reference values. Such a comparison can evaluate the performance of the measurement system and permit inferences to be made on the quality of the data for test samples.

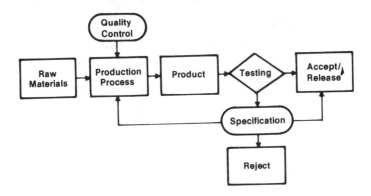

FIG. 1—*Production process quality assurance.*

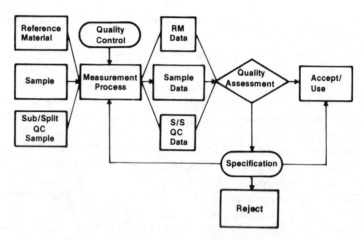

FIG. 2—*Measurement process quality assurance.*

Quality Control

Basic Elements

The experience of measurement experts, for example analytical chemists, dictates the techniques, operations, and laboratory practices necessary to obtain measurements of a given precision and accuracy. The basic elements of these are shown in Table 1 and will be briefly discussed.

Good laboratory practices (GLPs) denote the *modus operandi* that analytical chemists have developed to produce reliable measurements. They consist of general practices such as cleaning of laboratory ware, reagent control, environment control, sample handling, and maintenance of records, and practices unique to specific measurement techniques. GLPs are best developed and specified by the laboratory personnel involved on the basis of their own ex-

TABLE 1—*Basic elements of quality control.*

Good laboratory practices (GLPs)
   General practices
   Technique—Specific Practices
Standard operations procedures (SOPs)
Protocols for specific purposes (PSPs)
Education/training
   Formal
      Courses
      Seminars
   Informal
      Discussions
      Reading

perience and that of their peers. The GLPs should be documented for guidance of present and future laboratory personnel. Moreover, they should be reviewed periodically and up-dated as necessary.

Standard operations procedures (SOPs) describe the way specific operations and methods are performed. These include sampling operations, sample preparation, calibrations, measurement procedures, and in fact any operation that is done on a repetitive basis. "Standard" means that it specifies the way the operation is to be done, which may or may not be that developed by a standards-writing organization. However, when such are available, laboratories are well advised to adopt them since they represent peer judgment and provide a basis for comparability of data among user laboratories.

Protocols for specific purposes (PSPs) define the procedures to be followed in specific measurement situations such as a specific analytical or a monitoring program. They define the sampling program, specify the methodology to be used, the measurement sequences, the quality assurance plan, and the data validation and reduction procedures. PSPs may cite the laboratory's documented GLPs and SOPs as pertinent and available but should include any modifications required by the special circumstances of the specific test program.

Education and training are basic elements of any quality control program. Experience has shown that well informed and highly motivated personnel are key factors for good measurements. Management should support and encourage attendance at formal courses and seminars on specific measurement techniques, statistical concepts, and general aspects of quality assurance. In addition, informal training including reading and group discussions, has been found to provide helpful information on both metrological practices as well as on the goals and objectives of the specific laboratory. These tend to promote the philosophy to "think quality" and "quality as a way of life."

Basic Policy

The basic constituents of a quality control policy are outlined in Table 2. The laboratory should adopt a policy to use only qualified personnel in every critical operation. This means that every such person must be specifically trained for the tasks assigned and the competence to perform must be verified before he or she is permitted to produce definitive data. The use of reliable equipment means that such is suitable for the purpose, is in satisfactory condition, and is in calibration at the time of use. A good SOP should include a procedure to verify the operational condition of any equipment required before it may be used in a measurement program.

Measurements should be made using only approved methodology, demonstrated to be appropriate for the measurement problem by prior measurement of reliable reference samples. Strict adherence to SOPs and GLPs must be mandated by the laboratory management. The use of appropriate calibrations and standards cannot be overemphasized. Modern analysis consists largely in the

TABLE 2—*Basic quality control policy.*

Use of qualified personnel/operators
Use of reliable equipment
Use of approved methodology
Protocols for all critical steps/operations
Use of SOPs
Strict adherence to GLPs
Use of appropriate calibrations and standards
Close supervision of all operations by
management/senior personnel

comparison of unknowns with prepared standards. The reliability of the calibration process and the quality and suitability of the standards or calibrants or both is often critical to the quality of the data.

Close supervision of all operations by competent senior personnel is an important aspect of quality control. Built-in checks, review of data and reports, and a mechanism for real-time feedback to take corrective actions have been found to be effective means to monitor data quality and to detect and remedy difficulties before they become major problems.

Quality Assessment

Quality assessment techniques denote those ways by which the measurement process may be monitored in order to infer the quality of the data output. Table 3 summarizes a number of approaches that may be used. They are classified as internal or external, depending on the source of assistance needed to implement the assessment technique. Internal test samples may consist of internal reference materials, split samples, spiked samples, and surrogates which are measured in suitable test routines to evaluate the precision of the measurement pro-

TABLE 3—*Quality assessment techniques.*

Internal
Repetitive measurements
Internal test samples
Control charts
Interchange of operators
Interchange of equipment
Independent measurements
Audits
External
Collaborative tests
Exchange of samples
External reference materials (ERMs)
Standard reference materials (SRMs)
Audits

cess. These are best used in a control chart format [2] with capability of prompt response to any apparent problems.

Internal methods which may be used to check for or evaluate bias include interchange of operators and apparatus/equipment, and measurement of selected samples by independent techniques. This latter approach is especially useful when external aids, such as SRMs, are not available to evaluate bias.

Several procedures may be followed to provide external evidence of the quality of a measurement process. These can confirm the internal evaluation of precision and provide independent assessment of any bias (or lack thereof). Techniques include participation in collaborative test exercises, exchange of samples with other laboratories, and the analysis of reference materials obtained from external sources (ERMs). The National Bureau of Standards Standard Reference Materials (SRMs) are unexcelled as test materials to evaluate the measurement process when they are properly used [3,4].

From the foregoing discussion, it should be clear that every laboratory has within-house capability to estimate the precision of its measurements. The evaluation of bias is difficult, internally, but facilitated by the use of externally available techniques. No matter what the source of information, any evidences of malperformance, whether it be lack of precision or intolerable bias, should be carefully investigated and appropriate corrective actions should be taken as necessary. After such actions, follow-up measurements should be undertaken to verify that the problems have been eliminated.

Audits are listed as both internal and external quality assurance techniques. Two kinds of audits may be used. Systems audits consist of both systematic and spot checks of equipment, facilities, and procedures for compliance with the quality assurance plan. Performance audits depend on the use of test samples to evaluate laboratory proficiency. Monitoring networks and accrediting agencies often include audits as part of their procedures to evaluate laboratories. Laboratory management is well advised to develop its own auditing program and to conduct internal audits on both an announced and unannounced basis. Audits are only effective when a feed-back is established and used to correct any deficiencies that are identified.

Basic Responsibilities

A quality assurance program is only as effective as it is systematically implemented. Ordinarily, this means that a formal QA program must be established which documents the policy and the procedures to be followed, together with the various responsibilities for implementing them. In general, these responsibilities are as follows:

Upper management   establishes policy; provides resources to implement program; oversight.

Supervisory staff   implementation of the program; general supervision.

| *Technical staff* | technical competence to carry out daily operations; strict adherence to GLPs and SOPs; identification and correction of any technical defects in plan. |
| *Quality assurance coordinator* | oversight of QA program; advisory assistance to supervisory and technical staff; evaluation of effectiveness of QA program. |

Documentation

Measurement data must be technically sound and often it must be legally defensible in the broadest interpretation of the term. Accordingly, adequate documentation is a key requirement in all aspects of quality assurance. What was done, as well as how it was done, needs to be documented in an unambiguous and easily retrievable manner. This pertains to both the measurement process itself and the samples that were actually analyzed. A well-documented chain of custody ordinarily must be established and operated to ensure the integrity of the samples.

Other Aspects

The model of the problem investigated and the validity of the samples analyzed share equal importance with the measurement program. It is obvious that high quality measurements are of little consequence on defective samples. Likewise, an inappropriate model can require measurements and samples that are inapplicable to the problems of interest. The reader is referred to two earlier papers where the relation of such matters to data quality is discussed in some detail [1,5].

Benefits

A quality assurance program as outlined may appear costly, but this should be far outweighed by the benefits gained from its use. To the extent that statistical control is achieved, the measurement process may be considered as a production process with defined performance characteristics. Accordingly, the reliability of each measurement does not need to be individually demonstrated, but is assured by the process itself. Thus, each measurement supports every other measurement. A reliable basis for the assignment of measurement uncertainty is then established.

A measurement process under statistical control is evidently efficient, in that less replicates are required for the same or even greater reliability. Experience has also shown that less do-overs are required. The additional confidence inspired in the laboratory management, its staff, and the users of its data are intangible benefits.

References

[1] Taylor, J. K., *Analytical Chemistry*, Vol. 53, 1981, pp. 1588A-1596A,
[2] ASTM Manual on Presentation of Data and Control Chart Analysis, *STP 15D*, American Society for Testing and Materials, Philadelphia, Pa. 19103.
[3] Cali, J. P. et al., "The Role of Standard Reference Materials in Measurement Systems," NBS Monograph 148, National Bureau of Standards, Washington, D.C., Jan. 1975.
[4] Taylor, J. K., "Reference Materials—How They Are, or How They Should be Used," *ASTM Journal of Testing and Evaluation*, Vol. 11, 1983, p. 355.
[5] Kratochvil, Byron and Taylor, J. K., *Analytical Chemistry*, Vol. 53, 1981, pp. 924A-938A.

Gary L. Hensler[1]

An Introduction to Statistical and Ecological Software

REFERENCE: Hensler, G. L., **"An Introduction to Statistical and Ecological Software,"** *Statistics in the Environmental Sciences, ASTM STP 845*, S. M. Gertz and M. D. London, Eds., American Society for Testing and Materials, 1984, pp. 74–89.

ABSTRACT: An introduction to the readily available ecological software is given along with information on obtaining documentation and programs. General statistical software useful in ecological research is also considered; some references useful in comparing large statistical packages are given.

KEYWORDS: computer software, statistics, ecology

A biologist may be called upon to help answer many questions: (1) How many large mouth bass are there in a certain lake today, ten years after it was stocked?; (2) What is the size of the adult wood duck population in Illinois?; (3) How does ingestion of phosphamidon affect the growth rate of mallard ducklings?; (4) What environmental factors account for the species composition in a particular river basin's ecosystem, and how would installation of a nuclear power plant upstream affect this community?; (5) Of several release techniques, which is the most successful in reestablishing an endangered species from captivebred stock?

Statistical analyses can help provide these answers, and computer programs are often available to perform the complex analytical calculations. In particular, estimates of population size and density can be made using capture-mark-recapture or line transect methods. Capture-recapture techniques can also give estimates of such parameters as recruitment rates and age specific mortality rates. Community structure can be analyzed using a host of multivariate techniques relating environmental parameters to species composition or population sizes. Some of these techniques are principal components analysis,

[1]Biometrician, U.S. Fish and Wildlife Service, Patuxent Wildlife Research Center, Laurel, Md. 20708.

cluster analysis, correspondence analysis, and discriminant analysis. Additionally, environmental biologists may employ commonly used statistical techniques such as analysis of variance and simple linear regression.

The computer programs designed to perform these types of analyses can be called statistical and ecological software. This paper provides an introduction to some software of particular use to ecologists for which good documentation exists.

Much of the statistical software used in ecological studies was written for general statistical use in varied applications. Ecologists use the same regressions, analyses of variance, t-tests, etc. as do economists. Most computer support installations will offer a number of individual programs to do these analyses. In common to many computing installations, however, are the large statistical packages. These packages are collections of programs which can perform a variety of data management functions and statistical analyses on the same data set. They generally have similar control card formats for running all analyses within the package. The most widely used of these packages are SAS [1,2], BMDP [3], and SPSS [4,5], although many other packages are gaining widespread use.

In addition to general statistical software, statistical software expressly written for ecological programs is available. Included are programs to analyze data from line transects or capture-mark-recapture studies, or programs to calculate diversity and ordination statistics, or programs to estimate fish catch. These programs may apply techniques that are useful for other than ecological applications, but they use language in the documentation familiar to ecologists. Some of these ecological programs are discussed later. All quotes are from the respective user's manuals. Table 1 gives addresses where one may write for further information, complete documentation, or copies of the program.

Some Available Ecological Software

Line Transect Software

Line transect experiments estimate the density of biological populations based on sightings of members of a population by an observer moving along a transect. Models generally assume a distribution which gives the probability of sighting a member of the population at certain distances and angles to the transect. Typical distributions include triangular, half normal, exponential, and gamma. Nonparametric estimation of this distribution is also used.

TRANSECT, by Jeffrey L. Laake, Kenneth P. Burnham, and David R. Anderson, is a "comprehensive computer program which provides an analysis of line transect data for estimation of density." In addition to the User's Manual [6] there is a publication *Estimation of Density from Line Transect Sampling of Biological Populations* [7] giving the statistical and conceptual background for line transect sampling as well as field sampling procedures and study designs.

TABLE 1—*Address information for programs and documentation.*

---

1. TRANSECT by Laake, J. L., K. P. Burnham, and D. R. Anderson.
   User's Manual for Program TRANSECT, Utah State University Press, Logan, Utah 84322.
   Program tape from SHARE Program Library Agency, P. O. Box 12076, Research
   Triangle Park, N.C. 27709.
2. LINETRAN by Gates, C. E.
   LINETRAN User's Guide and Program from Dr. C. E. Gates, Institute of Statistics,
   Texas A&M University, College Station, Tex. 77843.
3. CAPTURE by White, G. C., K. P. Burnham, D. L. Otis, and D. R. Anderson.
   User's Manual for Program CAPTURE, Utah State University Press, Logan, Utah, 84322.
   Program tape from SHARE Program Library Agency, P. O. Box 12076, Research
   Triangle Park, N.C. 27709.
4. ESTIMATE and BROWNIE by Brownie, C., D. R. Anderson, K. P. Burnham, and
   D. S. Robson.
   Program and Handbook available from Chief, EDP Section, U.S. Fish and Wildlife
   Service, Patuxent Wildlife Research Center, Laurel, Md. 20708.
5. POPAN-2 by Arnason, N. A., and L. Baniuk.
   User's Manual and Program from Charles Babbage Research Center, Box 370, St.
   Pierre, Manitoba, Canada.
6. Method of Scoring Programs. Contact authors directly.
   White, G. C., Los Alamos Scientific Laboratory, LS-6, MS495, Los Alamos, N. Mex.
   87545.
   Conroy, Michael, U.S. Fish and Wildlife Service, Patuxent Wildlife Research Center,
   Laurel, Md. 20708.
   Burnham, K. P., U.S. Fish and Wildlife Service, Western Energy and Land Use Team,
   2627 Redwing Rd., Fort Collins, Colo. 80526-2899.
7. ONEPOP by Gross, J. E., J. E. Roelle, and G. I. Williams.
   Program and documentation from Colorado Cooperative Wildlife Research Unit,
   Colorado State University, Fort Collins, Colo. 85021.
8. RAMAS 1.0 by Ginzburg, L. R. and F. J. Rohlf.
   Program and documentation from Applied Biomathematics, Inc., 18 Camelot Lane,
   Setauket, N.Y. 11733.
9. Cedar Creek Software Library (CCSL).
   Programs and information from K. C. Zinnel, Dept. of Ecology and Behavior Biology,
   107 Zoology, 318 Church St., S.E., University of Minnesota, Minneapolis, Minn. 55455.
10. Radio Telemetry Software by Dunn, J. E.
   Programs and documentation from Dr. J. E. Dunn, Statistics Department, University of
   Arkansas, 3021 Sci-Eng Bldg., Fayetteville, Ark. 72701.
11. Radio Telemetry Movie Software by White, G. C.
   Program and documentation from Dr. G. C. White, Los Alamos Scientific Laboratory,
   LS-6 MS495, Los Alamos, N. Mex. 87545.
12. CEP (Cornell Ecology Program Series), Gauch, H. G., Ed.
   Program and documentation from Hugh G. Gauch, Jr., Ecology and Systematics,
   Cornell University, Ithaca, N.Y. 14853 (Tel. orders 607-256-3017).
13. NT/SYS by Rohlf, F. J., J. Kishpaugh, and D. Kirk.
   Program and User's Manual from Dr. James Rohlf, Department of Ecology and
   Evolution, The State University of New York at Stony Brook, Stony Brook, N.Y. 11794.
14. EAP by Smith, R. W.
   Programs and documentation from Dr. R. W. Smith, 1151 Avila Dr., Ojai, Calif. 93023.
15. CLUSTAN by Wishart, D.
   Program and User's Guide from Dr. David Wishart, Computer Center, University
   College London, 19 Gordon St., London, England WC1 HOAH.
16. DYNAMO by Forrester, J. W.
   Information from Dr. J. W. Forrester, Sloan School of Management, Massachusetts
   Institute of Technology, Cambridge, Mass. 02139.
17. MODAID by Kirchner, T.
   Information from Dr. Tom Kirchner, Natural Resource Ecology Lab, Colorado State
   University, Fort Collins, Colo. 80525.

TABLE 1—(*Continued*)

18. SIMCOMP by Gustafson, J. E.
    See Gustafson [21] for coding and details.
19. CSMP from IBM
    For ordering information contact local IBM marketing offices; available manuals include a descriptive flyer (G3201-6081), CSMP-III General Information Manual (GH19-7000), and APL-CSMP Program Description Operations Manual (SH20-21150).
20. Fisheries Software.
    Programs available from Fisheries Analysis Center, School of Fisheries WH-10, University of Washington, Seattle, Wash. 98195 (phone 206-543-9167).
21. FWS/MANAGE.
    For information write Creative Consulting Corporation, International, P. O. Box 1172, Fort Collins, Colo. 80522.
22. BMDP
    For ordering information call or write BMDP Statistical Software, P. O. Box 24 A 26, Los Angeles, Calif. 90024 (Tel. 213-825-5940 or 213-475-5700).
23. P-STAT
    For ordering information call or write P-STAT, Inc., P. O. Box 285, Princeton, N.J. 08540 (Tel. 609-924-9100).
24. SAS
    For ordering information call or write, SAS Institute, Inc., Box 8000, Cary, N.C. 27511-8000 (Tel. 919-467-8000 or Telex 802505).
25. SPSS
    For ordering information call or write, SPSS, Inc., Suite 3300, 444 N. Michigan Ave., Chicago, Ill. 60611 (Tel. 312-329-2400).

LINETRAN, by Charles E. Gates, is a "FORTRAN computer program that computes a variety of parametric and nonparametric estimators of density for the line transect method." An article giving the "theoretical background, justification, rationale and evaluation of many of these estimates" is given in Gates [8, 9].

Capture-Mark-Recapture Software

For these experiments, samples of n_i animals from a population are captured at times t_i ($i = 1, 2, \ldots, T$). The number of previously marked individuals in each sample is noted; the animals may then be marked or remarked and released. Histories of animals' captures and recaptures are used to estimate parameters such as population size, mortality rates, and recruitment rates. Different models result when one assumes a population which is open or closed to births (recruitment or immigration) or deaths (emigration) or both. In some models one can allow capture probabilities to vary over time or over the individuals in the population, or one can allow age-class structures in the populations. Special cases of capture-recapture experiments include band recovery models in which only harvested animals are recaptured (hence there is no remarking). For band recovery models population size cannot be estimated, but recruitment and mortality rates can be.

CAPTURE, by Gary C. White, Kenneth P. Burnham, David L. Otis, and David R. Anderson, is a FORTRAN program providing analyses of capture-mark-recapture data from eight closed population models [10]. These eight models arise from allowing capture probabilities to vary over time, by behavioral response, among individuals, or in combinations of these. Estimates of population size can be made in only five of these models, but all models can be assessed to find that model which best fits the data at hand. The Wildlife Monograph, *Statistical Inference From Capture Data on Closed Animal Populations* by Otis et al [11] provides detailed discussion of the fundamental concepts and of the eight models treated by the authors.

ESTIMATE and BROWNIE are FORTRAN programs for estimating survival and recovery rates in band recovery models. The discussion and examples focus on bird banding studies but are "potentially applicable to fish tagging experiments, entomological investigations, and studies of certain reptiles and amphibians." ESTIMATE handles models with one age class while BROWNIE handles those with two or three age classes. Fourteen models allowing survival and recovery rates to vary with sex of the bird, calendar year, banding history, or age class are considered, and a best fit can be found. A discussion of the models and the programs is in *Statistical Inference from Band Recovery Data—A Handbook* by Brownie et al [12].

POPAN-2, by A. Neil Arnason and Lee Baniuk [14], is "a data maintenance and analysis system for mark-recapture data" written in FORTRAN. POPAN-2 handles three open population models and one closed. It uses a general Jolly-Seber model (Jolly [14] and Seber [15]) allowing multiple recaptures and information on captured individuals that are not marked. It allows survival rates to vary over time, producing estimates of survival rates in addition to population size. POPAN-2 also has a data base management system.

Recently three programs were developed separately by Gary White (Los Alamos Scientific Lab), Michael Conroy (Patuxent Wildlife Research Center), and Kenneth Burnham (Western Energy and Land Use Team) which use numerical methods (primarily the method of scoring) to calculate maximum likelihood estimates for parameters from a general multinomial likelihood function. This technique has application to capture-recapture models, multiple age-class band recovery models, and survival models (especially from telemetry data). These programs will handle many of these models, but due to the programs' general approach more user input is required to specify the likelihood function.

Life Table Analysis Software

For life table analyses one inputs initial values for population parameters such as age class structure, mortality rates, birth rates, and population size. The programs then predict future states of the population. One can assess the effects on future generations of management decisions that may alter the initial parameters, or one can estimate parameters such as extinction probabilities. These programs are useful management tools.

ONEPOP, by Gross et al [16], is a life table simulation model designed to aid wildlife management agencies with planning and decision making processes concerning the husbandry of wildlife resources. It was put out in the early 1970s by the Colorado Cooperative Wildlife Research Unit. It can run in BASIC on rather small machines.

RAMAS 1.0 is an "age structured population analysis, risk assessment and management alternatives system" written by Lev R. Ginzburg and F. James Rohlf. It is a "micro computer based interactive package which allows the user to obtain future population characteristics for an arbitrary period of time accompanied by their 95% confidence limits." Parameters estimated with confidence intervals include the expected number of individuals in an age class and the expected time until population size reaches a preassigned level.

Radio Telemetry Software

Another area useful in ecological studies is that of radio telemetry animal tracking studies. Programs to analyze data from such studies are the Cedar Creek Software Library (CCSL) and programs written by James E. Dunn at the University of Arkansas. The CCSL edits and summarizes data; conducts basic home range analyses and cumulative home range analyses; calculates intensity of use and frequency of fixes; and analyzes randomness of movement and interactions between animals. Dr. Dunn's programs perform similar analyses, but he bases his calculations on the multivariate Ornstein-Uhlenbeck diffusion process which accounts for lack of independence of successive observations. In addition to these programs, Gary White (Los Alamos Scientific Laboratory) has software which generates movies from biotelemetry data. This program has special hardware and camera requirements.

Multivariate Analyses of Community Structure Software

Multivariate analyses of community ecology attempt to find structure among the numerous environmental variables of a biological community considered simultaneously. There are three basic multivariate strategies: (1) direct gradient analysis, (2) ordination, and (3) classification. Several computer packages are available to execute the often complex statistical techniques. Among the techniques used are principal components analysis, nonmetric multidimensional scaling, cluster analysis, discriminant analysis, and reciprocal averaging.

Perhaps the most widely used set of ecological software for analyses in community ecology is the Cornell Ecology Programs Series (CEP), edited by Hugh G. Gauch, Jr. The CEP series deals mainly with ordination and classification and is written in IBM's FORTRAN IV. Examples of programs in this series are: (1) GAUSSIAN ORDINATION, which performs Gaussian ordination of a species importance matrix; (2) ORDIFLEX, a program of four ordination techniques; weighted average, polar, principal components, and reciprocal averaging; (3) DECORANA, for detrended correspondence analysis. A companion book giving details on the analytical and statistical methodologies used in CEP is *Multivariate Analysis in Community Ecology*, Gauch [17].

NT/SYS is a numerical taxonomy system of multivariate statistical programs, by F. J. Rohlf, J. Kispauch, and D. Kirk. Procedures include clustering, ordination (principal components and nonmetric multidimensional scaling), and matrix manipulations and graphics programs.

The Ecological Analysis Package (EAP), by R. W. Smith, is a set of user written SAS procedures for use with SAS data sets for performing multivariate community structure analyses. There are procedures for cluster analysis, simple coordinate analysis polar ordination, discriminant analysis, matrix manipulations, graphics and others.

CLUSTAN by Wishart [18] is another package which, like NT/SYS, offers a wide range of classification techniques as well as some other multivariate and graphics programs. Coding (in BASIC) for still other ordination and classification programs can be found in *Multivariate Analysis in Vegetation Research, 2d. ed.*, Orlóci [19], and a FORTRAN package for ordination and classification with data management capabilities is given in Wildi and Orlóci [20]. Gauch [17] in the appendix lists several additional sources of programs which perform these multivariate analyses.

Dynamic Simulation Software

Many ecologists are involved in simulation modeling of ecological systems. Usually a specific modeling program must be designed for each system modeled. There are some simulation languages useful in writing these ecosystem modeling programs. Some of these are: DYNAMO, by J. W. Forrester, MODAID, by Tom Kirchner, SIMCOMP, by J. E. Gustafson [21], and CSMP (Continuous System Modelling Program), available from IBM systems.

These languages are based on Forrester's state variable flow models; the first three are for discrete time systems, and CSMP is for continuous time systems. For these simulation languages, the user supplies the description of the starting states of the system and equations which relate the states to future times. The programs then use the user-supplied equations to simulate the future state of the ecosystem giving estimates of user-selected parameters.

Some Fisheries Software

Although the software discussed previously is useful in both wildlife and fisheries research, there are some programs written specifically with fisheries applications in mind. The Fisheries Analysis Center at the University of Washington offers some ninety programs written in the last 15 years for use with fisheries data. "Some of these programs written for generalized data handling are now outdated in the sense that most of their functions can be performed by software packages such as SPSS, IMSL [22], Minitab (Ryan et al [23]) and the like." Many of the older programs will require updating to new compilers, and some of the more recent programs are not very portable to other systems. The programs are categorized into three sections: (a) Programs for generalized data handling; (b) Programs for a specific fisheries research project; and (c) Programs for general fisheries applications.

Examples of programs are: (a) Smoothing frequency curves; t-tests; histograms; regressions; (b) Chum egg analysis; computations of length, age, sex composition of Sockeye Salmon runs in Bristol Bay; (c) Fish respiration program; analysis of catch curves and mortality rates; Von Bertalanffy growth-in-length and tag data curve analyses and plots; mortality estimates from tag recoveries per unit of fishing effort.

Other fisheries programs are found in Pienaar and Thomson [24], Lee [25], and in Abramson [26].

Other Software

Roger H. Green in his book *Sampling Design and Statistical Methods for Environmental Biologists* [27] discusses in addition to some of the programs mentioned in this report other computer programs available to the environmental biologist. Also, the book *Computer Programming in Quantitative Biology* (Davies [28]) offers good introductory materials. There is a database management program, FWS/MANAGE, designed especially to handle wildlife species data. It has some simple statistical capabilities and is currently used in resource management for water quality monitoring data, wetland inventories, and biological surveys.

I am sure that many reading this section on ecological software will notice the absence of one of his or her favorite pieces of ecological software. I regret such omissions and would appreciate receiving copies of documentation for ecological software I have not mentioned.

General Statistical Packages

Ivor Francis in the book *Statistical Software a Comparative Review* [29] discusses and gives ratings by developers and users of over 70 statistical packages and programs. He provides a paradigm which is useful for comparing statistical software. The paradigm is based on the four questions given in Table 2. Answers to these questions can aid in selecting statistical software for a given problem.

For most users, however, there may not be a single package which is "best" for all potential applications. Unless one is able to become familiar with many packages and programs and has many packages available, he will probably want to pick the one or two packages that will best satisfy most of his needs. This is not an easy task. It is further complicated in that a user's needs may change, and packages are constantly being modified and improved. What may

TABLE 2—*A paradigm for evaluating statistical software.*

1. *Capabilities:* Was the program designed to help solve problems like mine?
   1.1 Processing and displaying data
      1.1.1 file building and manipulation
      1.1.2 editing
      1.1.3 data display
   1.2 Exploration and mathematical analysis of statistical data
2. *Portability:* Can the program be transported conveniently to my computer?
3. *Ease of learning and using:* Is the program sufficiently easy to learn and use that it will actually be useful in solving problems?
4. *Reliability:* Is the program maintained by some reliable organization, and has it been extensively tested for accuracy?

best satisfy data management and analytical needs today may not next year. Yet few of us have the time to keep abreast of all these changes on our own. There is a growing literature base on comparisons of computing packages and algorithms for statistical applications; see, for example, Francis et al [*30*].

Four statistical packages with which I have some familiarity will be briefly discussed next. I primarily use the SAS package which may explain any bias you may find in my reporting. I did not thoroughly evaluate all statistical software before arriving at the decision to use SAS. Indeed, such diverse elements as marketing by the SAS Institute, my working in close proximity to SAS promoters, and inertia contribute to my use of SAS. Other, more objective comparisons that you may wish to consider are also given.

The four packages compared are SAS, BMDP, SPSS, PSTAT (Buhler and Buhler [*31*]). The point of this exercise is to identify a few ways in which packages differ and not to provide a complete basis for comparison. Information on the User's Manuals for each of these packages is given in the references, and address information is in Table 1.

Development of BMDP was begun around 1961 at UCLA; the BMD initials reflect the initial emphasis of the programs to biomedical applications. It is written mostly in FORTRAN and is available on a wide variety of machines. The user's manual provides a great deal of documentation on the technical aspects of the calculations used.

SPSS, initially developed in 1965 at Stanford and now located in Chicago, is also written mostly in FORTRAN and is available in both batch and interactive modes on a wide variety of machines. The letters in this name stand for *S*tatistical *P*ackage for the *S*ocial *S*ciences, and social science applications were its first emphasis. Its user's manual tries to give more statistical background than do the others.

Development of SAS (Statistical Analysis System) was begun in 1966 with experimental design and analysis in mind. Planned agricultural experiments at North Carolina State University and the Southern Agricultural Experimental Stations influenced its origins. SAS is written in PLI and FORTRAN and runs both in batch and interactively, but only on IBM or IBM plug-compatible machines. This is an advantage in data management and a disadvantage in portability. The 1982 user's manual includes for the first time considerable technical and statistical detail, and it refers to statistical sources in the literature. It is assumed by most packages that you know the statistical requirements in advance of using a specific procedure.

PSTAT was developed at Princeton University (hence the "P" in the name); it has a very good data management, file maintenance system, and like SPSS, was initially intended mainly for social science statistics. It runs in both batch and interactive modes on a variety of computers. It is the most conversational package of the four. The current user's manual does not give much technical nor statistical detail, but a new manual is to be released in 1983.

For file building, editing, and data display SAS is a clear leader with PSTAT a close second. SPSS is doing more in this area and is coming out soon with a new version, SPSS-X, which reportedly will rival SAS and PSTAT in this area. SPSS has a "report" subprogram which is quite handy for data display. BMDP is not moving in the direction of improved data management.

All four are "correct" in their algorithms, that is, the computations are correctly done. The "accuracy" of the answers, however, depends in part on the number of bits used to store a value for the computer's arithmetic operations, and on the algorithm the program uses for the computations. In selecting a package, one should jointly consider the type of data, the size of a usual data set, the storage space available in the computer you are using, the number of bits used to store numbers, and the computing algorithms involved in a typical application.

Unless you are running on an IBM 360/370 computer (or plug-compatible machines such as Amdahl, Itel, CDC Omega, Magnuson, Ryad, etc.) under OS or OS/VS, you cannot run SAS. SAS is not very portable at this time. The other three packages are available on a wide variety of machines, although PSTAT is not as widely portable as are BMDP and SPSS. Potential users should check with these companies to see if a version can be supported on their particular computer.

All four packages are fairly easy to learn and use depending on how sophisticated a user you wish to become. Learning the data management capabilities of SAS, PSTAT, and SPSS involves learning a programming "language." As with most things, the more time you spend learning these packages, the more you will be able to do with them. Most companies offer courses on the use of their packages. As mentioned before, all four are reliable, and they are supported by generally helpful staffs.

Some systems allow access to several packages. For example one could use PSTAT to set up, edit, and maintain data files; these files could then be passed to BMDP or SPSS for analysis. The combination of PSTAT and BMDP offers a powerful package comparable to SAS and available on many machines. One can access BMDP and SPSS from SAS as well. Using a variety of packages may be an alternative you wish to consider.

I have included a table (Table 3) prepared with reference to a report by John J. Miller from George Mason University which lists many of the statistical procedures available in BMDP, PSTAT, SAS, and SPSS. The depth of coverage these procedures give in their output may vary considerably among packages. As one can see from the table a wide range of statistical procedures is available through these packages. SAS offers more analysis procedures than do the others; it is the most versatile. PSTAT has the smallest number of available statistical programs.

A complete evaluation of which package is "best" for ecological use would be beyond the scope of this paper. Heiberger [32] evaluated several ANOVA (Analysis of Variance) programs for flexibility with respect to the number and types of designs they could accommodate. He concluded that GENSTAT ANOVA and SAS.76 GLM were best. Comments by Armor, Frane, Norušis and Wang, and Payne following Heiberger's article point up the diversity of opinion on this one issue. In the comments, one finds SPSS and BMDP favored. These articles should indicate how difficult it is to design a single ANOVA package for all users.

Velleman and Welsch [33] discuss the production of regression diagnostics by some packages (Minitab, SAS, BMDP, SPSS, TROLL, LINWOOD). A subsequent comment by Nie and Norušis (1982) followed by a rejoinder by Velleman and Welsch and a reply by Nie and Norušis [34], indicate how controversial evaluation of packages can be.

These articles also indicate that there has been extensive evaluation of these packages already. As another example of such evaluations the Biometrics Unit of Cornell University has available a set of Annotated Computer Outputs for Analyses of Unbalanced Data (see Searle and Henderson [35-38] and Searle and Kershner [39]). There is a lot of literature available for use in the comparison of statistical software packages.

The area of micro- and desktop computers is a relatively new area for statistical computing which is becoming more important especially in field operations. Microcomputers capable of performing linear model analyses (3-way nested ANOVA, regression), nonlinear regressions, histograms, multivariate analyses (Cluster Analysis, PCA, Discriminant), time series analyses, and more are available for under $2000. This is a fast growing field (Boardman [40]); two years ago there were an estimated 53 000 desktop computers sold each month (McGovern [41]), and in its 3 January 1983, issue *Time* magazine estimates that 2.8 million personal computers were sold in 1982 by 100 companies for $4.9 billion.

I have had experience with a statistical package for Tektronix microcomputers (4050 series). Some of the programs in their package have been useful, and the graphics are often very helpful in data exploration. However, a uniform data entry and management system needs to be a part of any package, and it was not part of this tape-based system. This limited its use and made it

TABLE 3—*Some statistical analyses for which procedures (programs, subprograms) are available in the software packages listed. A + indicates that the package contains a procedure to perform the analysis. A (+) under SAS indicates the procedure is in the user supported supplemental library.*

Statistical Analyses	Software Packages			
	BMDP	P-STAT	SAS	SPSS
A. Descriptive Statistics				
1. Data checking and inspection	+	+	(+)	
2. Simple statistics (mean, variance, etc.)	+	+	+	+
3. Histograms	+	+	+	+
4. Frequencies	+	+	+	+
5. Exploratory Data Analyses	+	+	+	
(stem-leaf, box whisker, outliers, etc.)				
6. Ranks		+	+	
a. Normal scores	+	+	+	
7. Probability plots	+		+	
8. t-tests	+	+	+	+
B. Plots and Charts				
1. Histograms	+	+	+	+
2. Probability plots	+		+	
3. Scatter plots	+	+	+	+
4. Contour plots			+	
5. Mapping			+	
C. Analyses of Variance				
1. t-tests	+	+	+	+
2. One-way ANOVA and ANCOVA	+	+	+	+
3. Multi-way ANOVA and ANCOVA	+	+	+	+
4. Repeated measures	+	+	+	+
5. Nested factors	+	+	+	
6. Random and mixed models	+		+	
7. Multivariate ANOVA and ANCOVA	+	+	+	+
8. General linear modelling			+	
D. Regressions				
1. Simple and multiple linear	+	+	+	+
2. All possible subsets	+		+	
3. Stepwise	+	+	+	+
4. Weighted least squares	+		+	
5. Polynomial	+		+	
6. Ridge			+	
7. Principal components	+		+	
8. Response surface			+	
9. Least absolute value			(+)	
10. Logistic	+		(+)	
11. Nonlinear	+		+	
Derivative free nonlinear	+		+	
12. Time series	+		+	
E. Frequencies				
1. Two-way and multi-way tables	+	+	+	+
(with tests on two-way tables)				
2. Logistic regression	+		+	
3. General log linear models	+		+	
F. Correlations				
1. Pearson	+	+	+	+
2. Nonparametric	+	+	+	+

TABLE 3—(*Continued*)

Statistical Analyses	Software Packages			
	BMDP	P-STAT	SAS	SPSS
G. Nonparametric				
1. Correlations	+	+	+	+
2. One-way ANOVA	+	+	+	+
3. Ranking and rank scores		+	+	
4. Kolmogorov-Smirnoff			+	+
5. Runs				+
H. Survival analyses				
1. Cox model analyses	+		(+)	
2. Life tables	+		(+)	
3. Probit			+	
4. Sequential life testing			+	
I. Time Series				
1. Box-Jenkins (time domain)	+		+	+
2. Spectral analyses (frequency domain)	+		+	
3. Econometric time series regression			+	
4. Time series cross sectional regression			(+)	
5. Seasonally adjusted time series	+		+	
6. Multivariate time series			+	
J. Multivariate analyses				
1. Multivariate regressions	+		+	+
2. MANOVA and MANCOVA	+	+	+	+
3. Cluster analyses	+		+	
Nearest neighbor			+	
Variable clustering	+		+	
Cases clustering	+		+	
Dendograms (tree diagrams)	+		+	
4. Discriminant analyses	+	+	+	+
Stepwise	+	+	+	+
Nearest neighbor			+	
Canonical variates analysis	+		+	+
Quadratic discrimination			+	
5. Principal components analysis	+	+	+	
6. Partial correlations	+		+	+
7. Canonical correlations	+		+	+
8. Factor analyses	+	+	+	+
K. Other analyses				
1. Scaling				
Guttman			+	+
Multidimensional			(+)	
2. Item analyses and reliability			(+)	+
3. Planning randomized experiments			+	
4. Scoring from preference pairs	+			
5. Boolean factor analysis	+			
6. Inbreeding coefficients			(+)	
7. Percentiles (other than median and quartiles)	+		(+)	
8. Matrix operations and manipulations			+	

suitable only for single-purpose solutions, since one has to re-enter the data for each different analysis.

We can expect great advances in statistical software for microcomputers in the next few years. Already there are packages on the market for Apple computers which claim to rival the large packages. Micros make excellent use of graphics, and this combined with "user-friendliness" will make micros an invaluable tool for the statistician once appropriate high-quality software is available.

The titles in *The American Statistician*'s statistical computing section over the last several years indicate that the field of statistical computing is constantly changing. It is a field ripe with controversy as well. Which package is best for analyzing repeated-measures designs with covariates and unbalanced data? How should programs handle ANOVA's with missing cells? This introduction is by no means an in-depth analysis; it is one person's view and is clearly biased by limited experience. Yet it may serve as a beginning from which to explore statistical and ecological software.

NOTE—Since this paper was written (October 1983), there have been a number of advances and changes in many of the programs and packages mentioned. For the latest information on updated versions, portability, and revised manuals, contact the sources listed in Table 1.

Acknowledgments

I wish to thank David R. Anderson, Hugh G. Gauch, Paul H. Geissler, James D. Nichols, Woolcott Smith, Gary C. White, Ivor Francis, Steven Gertz, John Miller, Rebecca Perry, and Byron K. Williams for their help in preparing this manuscript.

References

[1] *SAS User's Guide: Statistics*, SAS Institute, Cary, N.C., 1982, pp. 1–584.

[2] *SAS User's Guide: Basics*, SAS Institute, Cary, N.C., 1982, pp. 1–923.

[3] Dixon, W. J., ed., *BMDP Statistical Software 1981*, University of California Press, Los Angeles, 1981, pp. 1–723.

[4] Nie, N. H., Hull, C. H., Jenkins, J. G., Steinbrenner, K., and Bent, D. H., *SPSS Statistical Package for the Social Sciences*, 2nd Edition, McGraw Hill, New York, 1970, pp. 1–6.

[5] Hull, C. H., and Nie, N. H., Eds., *SPSS Update 7–9*, McGraw Hill, New York, 1981, pp. 1–402.

[6] Laake, J. L., Burnham, K. P., and Anderson, D. R., *Users Manual for Program Transect*, Utah State University Press, Logan, Utah, 1979, pp. 1–26.

[7] Burnham, K. P., Anderson, D. R., and Laake, J. L., *Estimation of Density from Line Transect Sampling of Biological Populations*, Wildlife Monograph No. 72, Wildlife Society, 1980, pp. 1–202.

[8] Gates, C. E., "Line Transect and Related Issues," in *Sampling Biological Populations*, R. M. Cormack, G. P. Patil, and D. S. Robson, Eds., Satellite Program in Statistical Ecology, International Cooperative Publishing House, Fairfield, Md., 1979, pp. 71–154.

[9] Gates, C. E., *LINETRAN User's Guide*, Institute of Statistics, Texas A&M University, College Station, Tex., 1981, pp. 1–47.

[10] White, G. C., Burnham, K. P., Otis, D. L. and Anderson, D. R., *User's Manual for Program CAPTURE*, Utah State University Press, Logan, Utah, 1978, pp. 1–39.

[11] Otis, D. L., Burnham, K. P., White, G. C, and Anderson, D. R., *Statistical Inference from Capture Data on Closed Animal Populations*, Wildlife Monograph No. 62, Wildlife Society, 1978, pp. 1–135.

[12] Brownie, C., Anderson, D. R., Burnham, K. P., and Robson, D. S., *Statistical Inference from Band Recovery Data—A Handbook*, Resource Publication No. 131, U.S. Dept. of Interior, Washington, D.C., 1978, pp. 1–212.

[13] Arnason, A. N. and Baniuk, L., *POPAN-2 Data Maintenance and Analysis System for Mark-Recapture Data*, Charles Babbage Research Center, Manitoba, 1978, pp. 1–269.

[14] Jolly, G. M., "Explicit Estimates from Capture-Recapture Data with Both Death and Immigration: Stochastic Model," *Biometrika* 52, 1965, pp. 225–247.

[15] Seber, G. A. F., "A Note on the Multiple-Recapture Census," *Biometrika* 52, 1965, pp. 249–259.

[16] Gross, J. E., Roelle, J. E., and Williams, G. I., *Program ONEPOP and Information Processor: A Systems Modeling and Communications Project*, Colorado Cooperative Wildlife Research Unit, Colorado State University, Fort Collins, Colo., 1973, pp. 1–327.

[17] Gauch, H. G., *Multivariate Analysis in Community Ecology*, Cambridge University Press, Cambridge, 1982, pp. 1–298.

[18] Wishart, D., *CLUSTAN User's Manual, 3rd Edition*, Edinburgh University, Edinburgh, 1978.

[19] Orlóci, L., *Multivariate Analysis in Vegetation Research, 2nd Edition*, Dr. W. Junk, the Hague, 1978, pp. 348–435.

[20] Wildi, O. and Orlóci, L., *Management and Multivariate Analysis of Vegetation Data*, Swiss Federal Institute of Forestry Research, Birmensdorf, 1980.

[21] Gustafson, J. D., SIMCOMP 3.0, Appendix 1.A. in *Grassland Simulation Models*, ed. G. Innis, Ecological Studies, Vol. 26, Springer Verlag, New York, 1978, pp. 22–300.

[22] *IMSL Reference Manuals* (4 volumes), IMSL, Inc., Houston, 1982.

[23] Ryan, T. A., Joiner, B. L., and Ryan, B. F., *Minitab Reference Manual*, Duxbury Press, Boston, 1982, pp. 1–157.

[24] Pienaar, L. V. and Thomson, J. A., "Three Programs Used in Population Dynamics," WVONB-ALOMA-BHYLD (FORTRAN 1130), *Fisheries Research Board of Canada Technology Report 367*, 1973, pp. 1–33.

[25] Lee, P. J., "Multivariate Analysis for the Fisheries Biologist," *Fisheries Research Board of Canada Technical Report 244*, 1971, pp. 1–182.

[26] Abramson, N. J., "Computer Programs for Fish Stock Assessment," FAO (Food Agricultural Organization, U.N.) Fisheries Technical Paper 101, 1971, pp. 1–148.

[27] Green, R. H., *Sampling Design and Statistical Methods for Environmental Biologists*, Wiley, New York, 1979, pp. 141–146.

[28] Davies, R. G., *Computer Programming in Quantitative Biology*, Academic Press, New York, 1971, pp. 1–492.

[29] Francis, I., *Statistical Software A Comparative Review*, North Holland, New York, 1981, pp. 1–542.

[30] Francis, I., Heiberger, R. M., and Velleman, P. F., "Criteria and Considerations in the Evaluation of Statistical Program Packages," *The American Statistician*, Vol. 29, 1975, pp. 52–56.

[31] Buhler, S. and Buhler, P., *P-STAT User's Manual*, P-STAT Inc., Princeton, N.J., 1979, pp. 1–323.

[32] Heiberger, R. M., "The Specification of Experimental Designs to ANOVA Programs," *The American Statistician*, Vol. 35, No. 2, 1981, pp. 98–104; comments by Armor, D. J. (p. 104), Frane, J. W., (p. 105), Norušis, M. J. and Wang, C. M. (p. 106), and Payne, R. W. (p. 107), reply by Heiberger (p. 108).

[33] Velleman, P. F. and Welsch, R. F., "Efficient Computing of Regression Diagnostics," *The American Statistician*, Vol. 35, No. 4, 1981, pp. 234–242.

[34] Nie, N. H., and Norušis, M. J., "More on Evaluating Computer Programs," *The American Statistician*, Vol. 36, No. 2, 1982, p. 141; comments by Velleman, P. F. and Welsch, R. F. (p. 141), and a reply by Nie and Norušis (p. 141).

[35] Searle, S. R. and Henderson, H. V., "Annotated Computer Output for Analyses of Unbalanced Data: BMDP2V," Biometrics Unit Mimeo Series 662-M, Cornell University, Ithaca, N. Y., 1978, pp. 1–24.

[36] Searle, S. R. and Henderson, H. V., "Annotated Computer Output for Analyses of Unbalanced Data: GENSTAT ANOVA and Regression," Biometrics Unit Mimeo Series 644-M, Cornell University, Ithaca, N. Y., 1978, pp.1–75.

[37] Searle, S. R. and Henderson, H. V., "Annotated Computer Output for Analyses of Unbalanced Data: SAS GLM," Biometrics Unit Mimeo Series 641-M, Cornell University, Ithaca, N. Y., 1978, pp.1–67.

[38] Searle, S. R. and Henderson, H. V., "Annotated Computer Output for Analyses of Unbalanced Data: SAS HARVEY," Biometrics Unit Mimeo Series 659-M, Cornell University, Ithaca, N. Y., 1978, pp.1–59.

[39] Searle, S. R. and Kershner, R. R., "Annotated Computer Output for Analyses of Unbalanced Data: SPSS ANOVA," Biometrics Unit Mimeo Series 660-M, Cornell University, Ithaca, N. Y., 1978, pp.1–34.

[40] Boardman, T. J., "The Future of Statistical Computing on Desktop Computers," *The American Statistician*, Vol. 36, 1982, pp. 49–58.

[41] McGovern, P. J. (publisher), "*Review and Forecast—Industry Report: Electronic Data Processing—Desktop Computers*," International Data Corp., Waltham, Mass., 1980, pp. 23–24.

Woollcott Smith[1]

Design of Efficient Environmental Surveys Over Time

Time is the most valuable thing that man can spend
...Theophrastus (382-287 B.C.)

REFERENCE: Smith, W., **"Design of Efficient Environmental Surveys Over Time,"** *Statistics in the Environmental Sciences, ASTM STP 845*, S. M. Gertz and M. D. London, Eds., American Society for Testing and Materials, 1984, pp. 90-97.

ABSTRACT: Classical survey design and data analysis methods deal with observations at a single time point and cannot be applied directly to time series problems. This paper describes some recent work in the design of environmental surveys conducted over time. A method is given for finding the optimum number of times to repeat a survey over time. It is also shown how time series models can be used to evaluate the utility of base line surveys.

KEY WORDS: survey design, experimental design, intervention analysis, time series, environmental surveys

Most important questions about ecosystems concern the dynamic or time-varying properties of the system. For this reason most environmental surveys and ecological studies are carried out over time. The addition of new time points to a survey or experiment may be the most important factor in increasing cost. Although a great deal of good theoretical and applied work in the design of surveys and experiments over time now exists, little of this work has found its way into the actual practice of environmental science. The objective of this paper is to outline briefly this subject and to direct the reader to the important literature. This discussion will be illustrated with some specific environmental examples.

To introduce some basic ideas we consider some examples of the design problem over time. Suppose we are interested in estimating the mean phytoplankton density in some fixed area over the summer months. Phytoplankton

[1]Associate professor, Statistics Department, School of Business Administration, Temple University, Philadelphia, Pa. 19122.

density varies not only over space but also over time. Single time point surveys, efficiently constructed using standard methods (Saila et al [1], Kelley and McManus [2], Sokal and Rohlf [3]), can give us efficient designs for estimating plankton density at a point in time. However, they do not tell us about the value of repeating the survey over time. Of course, if one is working within fixed cost constraints, increasing the number of time points will imply less effort and consequently less accuracy at any one time point. Evaluating survey errors and determining the most efficient sampling frequency is one of the more common survey design problems. This problem is discussed in some detail in the section on Survey Design Over Time.

In many environmental studies we not only observe nature, as in the example previously mentioned, but we manipulate or alter parts of the natural system. We not only have some control over the sampling plan, but also we have at least limited control over the manipulation of the system. For example, if we wish to determine the effect of a power plant on the phytoplankton assemblage at a site in an estuary, or the effect of ocean dumping of chemicals, we have limited control over the size and timing of the experimental treatment. The experimental design question is: what combination of treatments and sampling plan can best be used to estimate the effect of the treatment on the natural system? In the next section we review some common time series methods that can be used to determine efficient experimental programs.

These problems are still poorly defined. Perhaps more important than the technical solution to these problems is the systematic procedure for defining the problem more precisely. Often when the problem is well defined, the optimum or nearly optimum designs will be easy to determine. There are three components to the design problem: (1) defining the precise question; (2) finding a reasonable model for the system under study; and finally (3) determining the constraints of the program in terms of limits in time, cost, and number of samples. Many environmental study programs that are faulted for their statistical design failed because they did not carefully define the three parts of the design problem. Once the problem is well defined, the statistical optimization of the survey or experimental design is never an insurmountable problem.

Statistical designs, like mathematical models, may serve more than one purpose. Like theoretical ecosystem models, statistical designs do not pretend to reflect all of the complexities of the real world: the logistics of sampling, biases in sampling procedures, etc. Rather, they serve as a way of thinking about the survey, describing its properties, and evaluating alternative strategies.

Survey Design Over Time

The fundamental difference between time series designs and more standard sampling designs is that the time series sampling model assumes that the process is correlated over space and time. One then takes advantage of this correlated structure to construct efficient designs. There is a large statistical literature on this subject [4–8]. Moss and Tasker's [9] review of hydrographic data network designs gives a good view of the state of the art in water quality studies.

This paper will not review this large and complex literature but rather present, in some detail, a particular example, the design of a survey to estimate the mean of a natural process fluctuating over time. The most critical part of the definition of the problem is determining exactly what kinds of questions the survey is to answer. In studies investigating the concentration of a pollutant in a water body, the mean concentration of the pollutant may be the most important property of the process. In other situations, such as studies of the thermal effects of a power plant, the maximum temperature fluctuation may be the most important property of the process. In still other cases we may be interested in estimating trends over time. Each question will yield a slightly different approach to the design problem. In the remainder of this section we give a simple example of a survey problem we have investigated [10]. The example involves a survey to estimate the mean of a time varying process and contains all of the steps in the analysis and design of a complex survey problem.

Suppose we are interested in the concentration of a pollutant or organisms in some defined area, for example, a site in an estuary. The concentration will have both spatial and temporal variation. In this example we will assume that the sampling strategy at a time point is to conduct a simple random survey consisting of n-observations, $x_{i,t}$; $i = 1, 2, \ldots n$. Let $u(t)$ denote the mean concentration at time t: the estimator of $u(t)$ is

$$\hat{u}(t) = \frac{1}{n} \sum_{i=1}^{n} x_{i,t}$$

And the standard error is just

$$\sigma_{\hat{u}} = \sigma/\sqrt{n} \tag{1}$$

where σ denotes the standard deviation of a single measurement. However, we are not interested in estimating $u(t)$, but rather its mean over some fixed time period $(0, T)$

$$\bar{u} = \frac{1}{T} \int_0^T u(t)dt \tag{2}$$

One might think of $\bar{u}$ as representing the mean concentration of a pollutant over a year.

A good sampling strategy in time is to divide the time interval $(0, T)$ into m equal intervals and sample at the midpoint of each interval, Tubilla [5]. Thus, the sampling time points are

$$t_i = 0.5 \, T/m + (i - 1)T/m, \qquad i = 1, 2, \ldots m$$

Using this sampling plan an estimator of u is

$$\hat{\bar{u}} = \frac{1}{m} \Sigma \hat{u}(t_i) \tag{3}$$

This completes the description of the general sampling setup.

We can now discuss more precisely the definition of the survey design problem. The parameter of the process we wish to estimate is the mean over the interval $(0, T)$, given by Eq 2. The constraints of the survey program are the fixed costs associated with sampling at a time point and the cost of analyzing each sample. The total cost of the survey is then

$$\text{cost} = b \cdot m + c \cdot m \cdot n \tag{4}$$

where b is the cost of obtaining a new time point, that is, boat cost for the day, transportation, crew cost, etc., and c is the cost of the analysis of a single sample. The number of time points, m, and the number of samples per time point, n, must be constrained so that the cost is below some fixed level.

To evaluate the survey error we need a more exact model of the random fluctuations in the process $u(t)$. For simplicity we will assume that the process is a stationary process with an exponential correlation function

$$C(x) = E(u(t) - \mu)(u(t + x) - \mu)$$
$$= C_0 e^{-\beta t} \tag{5}$$

where μ denotes the mean of the process $u(t)$. The decay rate β in the covariance function $C(x)$ can be thought of as the flow rate of a pollutant through the system. Thus, one can obtain some knowledge about the covariance function through theoretical calculations, rather than actually observing the time series $u(t)$.

If we assume that the process is stationary and has the exponential covariance function, Eq 5, then using standard methods from mathematical statistics one can obtain an expression for the variance of $\hat{\bar{u}}$ [5,6,10]. This expression is given by

$$\sigma_{\bar{u}}^2 = \sigma^2/m \cdot n + \sigma^2(m) \tag{6}$$

The two terms on the right in Eq 6 represent the two independent sources of error in the survey. The first term is the error due to random sampling error at a single time point. The second term, $\sigma(m)$, is the error due to the averaging over m discrete time points. Tubilla [5] gives this term for the general covariance function; in the special case that we are considering, one obtains

$$\sigma^2(m) = C_0 \left\{ \frac{1}{m} - \frac{2}{\beta T} \left(1 + \frac{U}{\beta T} \right) \right.$$

$$\left. + \frac{2}{V} \left[e^{-\beta T/m} \left(1 - \frac{U}{V} \right) + \frac{2}{\beta T} e^{-\beta T/2m} \cdot U \right] \right\} \qquad (7)$$

where

$$U = 1 - e^{-\beta T}$$

and

$$V = m(1 - e^{-\beta T/m})$$

The object of the design is to minimize Eq 7 subject to the cost constraints given by Eq 4. This is a simple form of the nonlinear integer programming problem. Although the general problem can be difficult, this problem with only two variables and one constraint can be solved numerically. One searches for the optimum number of time points, m, by calculating for each m the number of random survey points, n, that satisfies cost Eq 4, and then evaluating variance Eqs 6 and 7.

Figure 1, from Smith [10], gives a typical set of values from an environmental survey. In this example $\sigma = 1.04$, $C_0 = 0.27$, $b = 750$, and $c = 50$. The maximum cost of the survey was set at 50 000 dollars. For $\beta = 0$ the process is constant over the time period, and the optimum sampling plan is to concentrate all the effort on a single time point. For $\beta = 100$ the process varies rapidly over time and the minimum variance is achieved at approximately 32 sampling periods.

Obviously this is just one way that time series models can be introduced into sampling designs. One should again refer to the references at the beginning of this section for a more detailed view of these sampling designs.

Experimental Design Over Time

A second kind of time series design involves manipulation of the environment, that is, a treatment. The experimenter can then design the treatment time series so as to obtain the most information about the effect of the treatment on the system.

The expected mean squared error for different sampling plans
with a fixed cost of $50,000.00. The fixed cost determines
the maximum number of samples (solid line) given the number
of sampling periods.

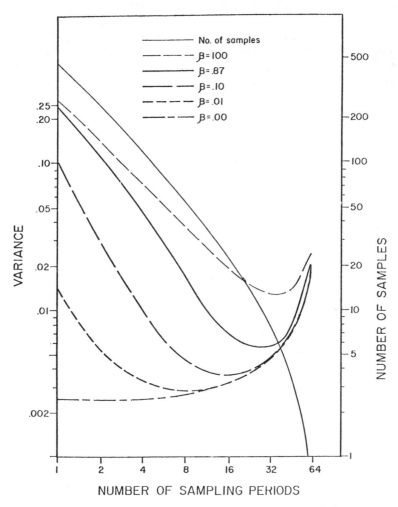

FIG. 1—*Typical set of values from an environmental survey* [10].

One widely used approach to the design of these kinds of experiments is to
use an extension of the autoregressive moving average (ARIMA) models, Box
and Jenkins [11]. This extension, called intervention analysis, Box and Tiao
[12], allows one to estimate the magnitude of an effect if the general shape of
the response function over time is known. The rather complex analytic methods yield estimators for the magnitude of the intervention as well as for the
estimation error. With these analytic results one can begin to investigate a

rather different set of design problems than those discussed previously. A thorough account of ARIMA designs is given in Glass and Gottman [13].

Consider the problem of designing an efficient environmental survey to determine the effect of a power generating plant with a once-through cooling system. Assume the power plant is scheduled to start operation in three years. The kinds of survey questions we might answer are: how much effort should be put into base line surveys before the plant starts operation, and how long should the survey continue after the plant starts operation. Using ARIMA methods, Lettenmaier, Hipel, and McLeod [14] investigated just this design problem for environmental impact studies. Their conclusion was that the ability of a design to detect an impact (that is, the statistical power) was very sensitive to the time allocated to the pre- and post-operation periods. However, it also depended on shape of the response. For example, they found that in the case where the intervention has an immediate effect which decays exponentially over time, the impulse decay function, the power of the survey is relatively insensitive to the number of survey points in the pre-intervention period. This kind of impulse response might be found in chemical and oil spill events. This is fortunate since pre-intervention surveys are least likely in this kind of situation.

However, in the case where there is no decay of the effect over time, that is a step response, the optimum pattern for the survey time points would be to allocate an equal number to pre- and post-surveys. The step function response approximately describes the response of a natural system to a power plant or other intervention where there is a constant impact after the initial change.

There are many other approaches to the design of experiments over time. In many cases the question asked about ecological impacts can be put into the framework of estimating parameters of nonlinear systems. In these cases the theory of nonlinear design is well worked out, Box and Lucas [15], and computer programs have been written to optimize the time point pattern; for example the NONLIN system [16], used primarily in pharmokinetic studies. Still another approach is outlined in Moore [17], where linear filtering theory is used to evaluate water quality sampling plans.

Classical experimental designs such as latin squares and randomized block design can be also modified to analyze effect and error terms correlated with time. Blaisdell and Raghavarao [17] and Afsarinejad and Hedayat [18] give an introduction to this literature.

Time series designs use the same basic theory as classical survey and experimental designs. The analysis of these problems is slightly more complex, but it should be well within the technical skill of the environmental scientists and planners. We know from repeated experience the costs and delays associated with poorly designed environmental programs. In comparison to these costs the added effort in carefully evaluating alternative time series designs is small.

References

[1] Saila, S. B., Pikanowski, R. A. and Vaughan, D. S., *Estuarine and Coastal Marine Science*, Vol. 4, 1976, pp. 119-128.

[2] Kelley, J. C. and McManus, D. A., *Marine Geology*, Vol. 7, 1969, pp. 465-471.

[3] Sokal, R. R. and Rohlf, F. J., *Biometry: The Principals and Practice of Statistics in Biological Research*, W. H. Freeman and Company, San Francisco, 1969, p. 376.

[4] Scott, A. J. and Smith, T. M. F., *Journal of the American Statistical Association*, Vol. 69, 1974, pp. 674-678.

[5] Tubilla, A., "Error Convergence Rates for Estimates of Multidimensional Integrals of Random Functions," Department of Statistics, Stanford University Technical Report No. 72, 1975.

[6] Cochran, W. G., *Annals of Mathematical Statistics*, Vol. 17, 1946, pp. 164-177.

[7] Schoenfelder, C. and Cambanis, S., *Annals of Statistics*, Vol. 10, 1982, pp. 526-538.

[8] Eubank, R., Smith, P. and Smith, P., *Annals of Statistics*, Vol. 9, 1981, pp. 486-493.

[9] Moss, M. E. and Tasker, C. D., *Review of Geophysics and Space Physics*, Vol. 17, 1979, pp. 1298-1306.

[10] Smith, Woollcott, *Estuarine and Coastal Marine Science*, Vol. 6, 1978, pp. 217-224.

[11] Box, G. E. P. and Jenkins, G. M., *Time Series Analysis Forecasting and Control*, Holden-Day, San Francisco, 1970, p. 553.

[12] Box, G. E. P. and Tiao, G. C., *Journal of the American Statistical Association*, Vol. 70, 1975, pp. 70-79.

[13] Glass, V., Wilson, V. L., and Gottman, J. M., *Design and Analysis of Time Series Experiments*, Colorado Associated University Press, Boulder, Colo., 1975, p. 300.

[14] Lettenmaier, D. P., Hipel, K. W., and McLeod, A. I., *Environmental Management*, Vol. 2, 1978, pp. 537-554.

[15] Box, G. E. P. and Lucas, H. L., *Biometrika*, Vol. 26, 1959, pp. 77-99.

[16] Metzler, G. M., Elfring, G. L., and McEwen, A. S., *Biometrics*, Vol. 30, 1974, pp. 562-570.

[17] Moore, S. F., *Journal of Hydraulics Division, Proceedings*, American Society of Civil Engineers, Vol. 99, No. HY5, 1973, pp. 815-831.

[18] Blaisdell, Ernest A. and Raghavarao, D., *Journal of the Royal Statistical Society Series B*, Vol. 42, 1980, pp. 332-338.

[19] Afsarinejad, K. and Hedayat, A., "Repeated Measurements Designs, II: Characterization, Construction, and Optimality," unpublished manuscript, 1975.

G. P. Patil[1]

A Proposed Cooperative Program on Statistical Ecology and Environmental Statistics for Increased Resource Productivity and Environmental Protection and the Panel Discussion at the ASTM Symposium on Statistics in the Environmental Sciences*

REFERENCE: Patil, G. P., **"A Proposed Cooperative Program on Statistical Ecology and Environmental Statistics for Increased Resource Productivity and Environmental Protection and the Panel Discussion at the ASTM Symposium on Statistics in the Environmental Sciences,"** *Statistics in the Environmental Sciences, ASTM STP 845*, S. M. Gertz and M. D. London, Eds., American Society for Testing and Materials, 1984, pp. 98–112.

ABSTRACT: The ASTM Symposium on Statistics in Environmental Sciences appeared to be an appropriate forum for an effective dialogue for agencies, industries, and academia to do something together that should be timely, fruitful, and synergistic. A panel discussion on a much needed cooperative program on statistical ecology and environmental statistics for increased resource productivity and environmental protection was organized for the morning of the second day of the symposium program. The present article is especially prepared to report on the session with multifaceted discussion for the benefit of the wider readership.

The proposed cooperative program considers formulation of prototype and experimental programs, such as, cooperative centers for statistical ecology and environmental statistics to conduct collaborative research on contemporary quantitative studies and issues in statistical ecology and environmental statistics involving scientific and public policy research. The proposed cooperative program also needs to formulate mechanisms for effective communication and continuing dialogue, such as, a quarterly scientific newsletter, timely symposia and workshops, satellite courses, and conferences with emphasis on contemporary quantitative studies and issues in statistical ecology and environmental statistics.

*This paper was prepared while the author was under partial support from the National Marine Fisheries Service on a project entitled, Stochastics and Statistics in Marine Fisheries Research and Management, under contract NA-80-FAC-00040.
[1]Professor of Mathematical Statistics, Department of Statistics and the Graduate Program in Ecology, The Pennsylvania State University, University Park, Pa. 16802.

KEY WORDS: statistical ecology, environmental statistics, resource productivity, environmental protection, cooperative research program, cooperative information transfer program, panel discussion

The ASTM Symposium on Statistics in Environmental Sciences appeared to be an appropriate forum for an effective dialogue for agencies, industries, and academia to do something together that should be timely, fruitful, and synergistic. A panel discussion on a much needed cooperative program on statistical ecology and environmental statistics for increased resource productivity and environmental protection was organized for the morning of the second day of the symposium program. Professor G. P. Patil was invited to be the moderator. Drs. Bradford Brown, Ella Filippone, Steven Gertz, Lev Ginzburg, Gary Hensler, Robert Lewis, and Woollcott Smith served on the panel to discuss the cooperative program as suggested by Professor Patil.

To speak of the participants that took part in the panel discussion, Dr. G. P. Patil is Professor of Mathematical Statistics at the Pennsylvania State University, and serves as the Chairman of the International Statistical Ecology Program. Dr. Bradford Brown is Chief of the Resource Assessment Division of the Northeast Fisheries Center at Woods Hole. Dr. Ella Filippone is the Executive Administrator of the Passaic River Coalition. Dr. Steven Gertz is the Manager of the Life Systems Department at Roy F. Weston, Inc., Philadelphia. Dr. Lev Ginzburg is Professor of Ecology at the State University of New York at Stony Brook. Dr. Gary Hensler is Mathematical Statistician at the Patuxent Wildlife Research Center of the Fish and Wildlife Service. Dr. Robert Lewis is Professor and Director at the Institute of Biogeography of the University of Saarland in West Germany. Dr. Woollcott Smith is Director of the Data Analysis Laboratory of the Department of Statistics at Temple University.

The present article is specially prepared to report on the session with multifaceted discussion for the benefit of the wider readership of this volume. Should you also like to offer your comments and suggestions, you are requested to send them to Professor Patil as soon as you can.

Background and Motivation

G. P. Patil—In my presentation yesterday of some of the perspectives of statistical ecology and environmental statistics, we saw a brief review of statistics, ecology, and environment in their broad context of science, technology, and society. It is important that a working framework is formulated so that industries, agencies, and academia get to effectively collaborate on issues, concepts, methods, and solutions that are intrinsically of a quantitative nature, regardless of the kinds of statistical uncertainties involved.

The following three excerpts on research and management of environment and natural resources should quickly help drive the need home.

Russell Train (1973) Administrator of the United States Environmental Protection Agency.

". . . For top management and general public policy development, monitoring data must be shaped into easy-to-understand indices that aggregate data into understandable forms. I am convinced that much greater effort must be placed on the development of better monitoring systems and indices than we have in the past. Failure to do so will result in suboptimum achievement of goals at much greater expense . . ." —from the United States Environmental Protection Agency, Washington, D.C., National Conference on Managing the Environment.

John Cantlon (1981) Chairman, TIE/HRI Study Panel.

". . . Our report is optimistic. It maintains that we have the potential to enhance the biological productivity required to meet our own needs for food and fiber and to assist other nations to meet theirs. To accomplish this increased productivity, however, we foresee the need for at least a doubling of research in the natural resources and environment sector. We believe these productivity needs are sufficiently imperative to recommend research augmentation, even during this time of essential fiscal austerity . . .

In the management of renewable resources, modeling serves to provide insight and guidance, to facilitate prediction and to define options for management and control . . .

The resource system modelers need to become conversant not only with the classical approaches to dynamic systems, but with modern approaches to ordinary and partial differential equations, stochastic processes, stochastic adaptive control theory, and statistical decision theory . . .

To project future trends and to deal adequately with the management of world resources, much more sophisticated tools are essential; this can only be achieved via a major commitment on the part of funding agencies to the training of environmental and resource systems modelers and the support of interdisciplinary research in the modeling and prediction of resource systems."—from the report on Productivity of Resources and Environments: A National Assessment of Research Trends and Needs, by the Institute of Ecology and Holcomb Research Institute.

Richard C. Hennemuth (1980) Acting Director, Northeast Fisheries Center.

". . . How do we get there? . . . The scientific information presented is in many cases so opaque that it comes down to a matter of demanding that the interested parties 'trust' the scientists. Rather than this, we must generate a climate of acceptability. The state of the natural systems we deal with must be described in credible terms. Scientific data insofar as humanly possible must jibe with the practical perceptions of the public and private users.

Only a part of this problem is solved by better writing. The real solution lies in a better understanding on the part of scientists themselves of what the observations are really measuring, and a clear way of expressing this.

These two considerations involve the underlying distributive properties of the variable we are observing and the ecological relations amongst the different variables.

Both of these aspects are included in statistical ecology which is now moving out of its classical phase and barren formalism.

The initiative would support studies of the distributional properties of fish, shellfish, plankton, etc., and also of the physical abiotic variables . . ."—from a Personal Communication on Statistical Ecology Intiative.

Now, the following three excerpts should help develop some feeling for certain basic issues and approaches regarding research, training, and management involving statistical ecology and environmental statistics.

John Skellam (1972): A Friend, Philosopher, and Guide.

"Mathematical ecology is moving out of its classical phase carrying with it untold promise for the future, but, as H. A. L. Fisher, the historian, remarks, progress is not a law of nature. Without enlightenment and eternal vigilance on the part of both ecologists and mathematicians there always lurks the danger that mathematical ecology might enter a dark age of barren formalism, fostered by an excessive faith in the magic of mathematics, blind acceptance of methodological dogma and worship of the new electronic gods. It is up to all of us to ensure that this does not happen . . ."—from some philosphical aspects of mathematical modeling in empirical science with special reference to ecology, In *Mathematical Models in Ecology*, J. N. R. Jeffers, Ed.

J. Stuart Hunter (1977): Incorporating Uncertainty into Environmental Regulations.

". . . The establishment of environmental guidelines and standards continues to be a major activity of EPA. . . . The establishment of environmental guidelines and standards has proved to be an iterative process. . . . In many cases, the Agency lacks data of adequate quality and quantity to be useful for establishing regulations. With such poor raw material, the ability of the Agency to progress much beyond the simplest applications of statistical methods is limited. However, as new and better data resources become available, as a consequence of the Agency's quality assurance programs, the Agency will wish to apply better modes of statistical analysis. The Agency should prepare for these future events by establishing centers of excellence in both the practice and theory of statistics.

Simultaneously, the Agency should use its current scant statistical resources only to solve these problems identified as most important to the Agency. This may require separating statistical needs into activities to be performed in-house, and those to be handled by outside statisticians. For example, we can imagine special in-house efforts in the establishment of regulations and environmental modeling, in forensic statistics, and in quality assurance, while the technical considerations of establishing sampling networks and protocols, the study of the influence of departures from statistical assumptions, and the adaptation of multivariate and time series methodologies to environmental problems might be contracted out to various universities or groups with special statistical expertise.

The Agency should take a more global view of its statistical needs and responsibilities and prepare for vigorous, organized growth."—from Environmental Monitoring, A Report to the EPA from the Study Group on Environmental Monitoring, National Academy of Sciences, Washington, DC.

G. P. Patil (1981): Interdisciplinary Research and Training.

"A student, a budding scientist, wishes to study 'Martian Philosophy,' but finds that there is no instructional program available in Martian Philosophy. He is advised to take courses in astronomy, which may have some bearing upon Mars; he is also asked to take courses in philosophy that may have some context of the universe; and in due course, he is declared to have completed a program in Martian Philosophy! The inadequacy of this approach is clear. It would be important to make sure that neither the student nor the supervisor falls into this trap. Integrated and interactive research training programs should be made available to those interested and concerned."—from Some Perspectives in Statistical Ecology, in *Ecologia*, 1, A. Moroni, O. Ravera, and A. Anelli, Eds.

A Proposed Cooperative Program

Any substantive program involves creation and communication of relevant information and knowledge. It amounts to a fruitful research effort and productive information transfer. The proposed cooperative program considers formulation of prototype and experimental programs, such as, cooperative centers for statistical ecology and environmental statistics to conduct collaborative research on contemporary quantitative studies and issues in statistical ecology and environmental statistics involving scientific and public policy research. The proposed cooperative program also needs to formulate mechanisms for effective communication and continuing dialogue, such as, a quarterly scientific newsletter, timely symposia and workshops, satellite courses, and conferences with emphasis on contemporary quantitative studies and issues in statistical ecology and environmental statistics.

Interdisciplinary efforts by several professional organizations have been instrumental in the promotion of scientific dialogues and in the dissemination of the results in a variety of published forms. The Committee on Statistics and the Environment of the American Statistical Association, the SIAM Institute for Mathematics and Society, the Mathematical Ecology Group in Great Britain, and the International Statistical Ecology Program, among others, come to mind in this connection. A list of the published volumes is included in the references at the end of this paper for the ready convenience of the ASTM reader.

A Proposed Cooperative Research Program

The proposed cooperative research program is envisaged in terms of various inhouse groups and centers with central cooperative research center. (Major responsibility and emphasis would have to be on quantitative issues and investigations of contemporary concern involving uncertainties in ecological and environmental problems). A typical cooperative research center would serve a four-point function, (a) Quantitative Arm, (b) Think Tank, (c) Information Transfer, and (d) a Nerve Center and Common Forum, for otherwise disparate ecologies and environments. To be able to meet this responsibility the Center would need effective interdisciplinary teams of energetic individuals and devoted professionals with a sense of strong commitment and continuity in the cause of the triangular trinity of statistics, ecology, and environment. To be logistically feasible and fruitful, the Center should have three to five year tenures subject to periodic reviews.

A scenario for a typical Center on a university campus would be expected to have features, such as:

(a) Ecology and environmental studies program option in quantitative ecology.
(b) Statistics program option in ecometrics and environmetrics.
(c) Campus-wide statistical ecology and environmental statistics group.
(d) Statistical ecology and environmental statistics spectrum course.
(e) Quantitative studies and issues research seminar.
(f) Role of quantitative arm, think tank, and information transfer for on and off campus sponsors.
(g) Summer institutes and courses.
(h) Center to concentrate on three to five research themes with well integrated interdisciplinary research teams.
(i) One of the Centers to host the information transfer program headquarters.
(j) University goodwill and support for the interdisciplinary program.

A proposed thematic working approach in the Center on a university campus would typically formulate problem themes and the corresponding research teams in close collaboration with the potential sponsor(s). Each research team would preferably command the following makeup: the principal investigator; quantitative ecology personnel consisting of a faculty associate, doctoral student, and a masters student; statistical personnel consisting of a committed statistician, doctoral student, and a masters student; and, the sponsoring agency/industry personnel consisting of the sponsoring scientist and the sponsoring manager. The team would need usual logistical support and facilities. Estimated budget level might be of the order of $50 to 100 K/year to be shared by the sponsor(s) and the university. It would be extremely desirable, almost essential, that about three year plans are made between the university and the sponsoring agency or industry or both.

A Proposed Cooperative Information Transfer Program

The proposed cooperative information transfer program is envisaged in terms of the following three-point function, (a) scientific quarterly newsletter with emphasis on scientific communication and dialogue on contemporary research, training, and public policy involving quantitative issues, (b) satellite program of courses and conferences with emphasis on short courses or conferences or both immediately before or after large conventions of relevant professional societies, and (c) semiannual symposia and workshops on timely topics of the year. An ongoing feature would be to invite sponsors to send representative(s) to participate in each one of the (a), (b), and (c).

The scientific quarterly newsletter would be expected to have a variety of features, such as:

(a) News items, advertisements for positions, RFPs.
(b) Questions-answers, letters, correspondence.
(c) Current publications, reports.
(d) Book reviews, report reviews.
(e) Research interests, needs, advances.
(f) Research in progress.
(g) Training programs, degree programs, and related activities.
(h) Conferences, courses, workshops, symposia.
(i) Issues and investigations with emphasis on methods, concepts, tools, areas of concern, policy issues, and related concerns.
(j) Subject area forums.
(k) Individual agency and industry forums.
(l) Software advances and needs.
(m) Short articles/and discussions.

An estimated budget of $100 K/year is expected to cover the minimal needs involving secretarial, communication, supplies, newsletter production, computer-related costs, printing service production of 1000 to 1500 copies of four issues a year, two topical semiannual symposia, and some of the professional time at the program headquarters. The needed resources may be explored with potential sponsor and cosponsors, founding sponsors, institutional sponsors, individual sponsors, institutional subscribers, individual subscribers, and student subscribers. It should be fruitful and timely to assess the long term interest and feasibility of the proposed information transfer program for statistical ecology and environmental statistics.

Panel Discussion

After his introductory remarks, Professor Patil invited the panelists to offer their comments and suggestions on the proposed cooperative program. The members of the panel responded as follows. Floor discussion followed thereafter, and the session adjourned with a sense of future purpose and forward look.

Panel Discussion Contributions by the Panelists

Bradford Brown (Northeast Fisheries Center, Woods Hole, Mass.).

This is both the worst of times and the most opportune of times to discuss a proposed new cooperative program in statistical ecology. It is the worst of times because no longer can merely the proposal of an effort that has sound scientific merit guarantee a high likelihood of federal funding on new monies. Furthermore within the Federal government this is a time of great uncertainty. There is great debate as to what the role of the Federal government in environmental and resource management issues should be. It is a time of great financial uncertainty; budgets not being passed and emergency resolutions allowing funding at the last minute for only small portions of the year and on and on.

It is also the most opportune time as those of us who are concerned about environmental and resource science look very interspectively at the efforts we have been making. We need to examine new ways to make our limited dollars go further in finding solutions to the problems facing us in these areas. We realize that any funding for a cooperative program will likely only come by taking funds away from other works in this area. At the same time the environmental/resource area is also competing with other areas in the spending dollar.

My conclusion is that only through increased efforts in applying the science of probability and the art of applied statistics to our environmental and resource problems can we hope to increase our efficiency in our regular operations and seek to define important new truths concerning these areas. To date much of the work in statistical ecology has been patchy. A few scattered people attempting to address themselves to this amongst a myriad of other duties. Thanks to Professor Patil there has been a major effort to bring these individuals together and to bring resource oriented subject matter specialists together with statisticians interested in research in this area.

One reason that we may not have been making as much progress as we would desire is that we have not assembled a critical mass of individuals to work on statistical ecology. The cooperative program does provide the concentration of effort that may give us breakthroughs. In order to be effective, however, it must not be limited solely to individuals in one location. It must be able to reach out to those people working in other institutions, encompass their work, involve them in team research, and provide the interactive and supportive situations so that all talents can be used to address these problems.

We must first and foremost keep the real life situation in mind. Ecological problems are extremely difficult. It is one thing to sample from a table of random numbers. I am still trying to get Professor Patil to experience the back deck of fisheries research vessel in heavy seas with the deck icing, at 3 a.m. in the morning towards the end of a three week cruise working 12 h a day, six on, six off.

Gary Hensler (Fish and Wildlife Service, Laurel, Md.).

At present there are not enough qualified statisticians in the areas of statistical ecology not concerned with human health. For the past three years I have organized sessions in wildlife and fisheries statistics at the Joint Statistical Meetings of the American Statistical Association (ASA), the Biometrics Society, and the Institute of Mathematical Statistics (IMS). Attendance at these sessions has not been high. We in statistical ecology face a real problem in educating and interesting other statisticians in our problems. Campus research centers such as those proposed for the cooperative program could serve to offer the courses and the research base to draw many more statisticians and mathematicians into ecological research. These centers could certainly help promote interdisciplinary research, breaking down barriers among ecologists, statisticians, and mathematicians, and between academia and industry.

Recognizing that ecological problems are often international in scope, statistical ecologists worldwide could greatly benefit from the proposed quarterly newsletter in that we could avoid duplicate effort and could learn from others' mistakes and others' solutions. Much of this information is now published in diverse places from international statistical journals to in-house industrial reports. The collection of titles pertinent to ecology would further the research effort.

But research is not enough. Environmental models may predict the long term adverse effect on world climates of destruction of forests in Latin America. The real problem comes in policy. How do we tell an overpopulated country with severe economic problems to sacrifice short-term economic gains for long-term environmental protection? The proposed cooperative program must involve itself in public policy research and public policy decision making. We must not be content with research that merely points to environmental problems, but rather we must offer solutions that can effect a positive impact on the world's environment while considering the real problems faced by many of the world's people. Difficult problems must be confronted and choices made; we should not allow these choices to be made without knowledge of the best available environmental research and policy research results. The proposed international cooperative program should intend to involve itself whenever and wherever possible in these management decisions.

Woollcott Smith (Temple University, Philadelphia, Pa. Formerly of Woods Hole Oceanographic Institution).

The central problem in all of statistics is to understand, analyze, and make more efficient the decision making process. Professor Patil and other statisticians working on environmental and ecological problems are relating this fundamental approach to one of the more important decision problems our society now faces.

Decision making on environmental issues is imperfect. Although there is room for considerable progress, statisticians must recognize that many important environmental problems cannot be placed in the classical statistical framework. A careful and innovative analysis of these problems will certainly lead to new theoretical and practical results.

Environmental statistics is not a separate and isolated field, but rather is central to the theory and practice of a number of academic disciplines including ecology, economics, and statistics. The cooperative program that Professor Patil proposes recognizes and takes advantage of this. It will be an efficient forum for the development of practical solutions to some of the pressing problems in environmental monitoring and regulation and will provide new theoretical approaches to some of these problems.

Lev Ginzburg (State University of New York at Stony Brook, N.Y.).

I fully support the idea of the proposed cooperative program. Most of what I would like to say has been said before. The only additional comment that I have is that I feel that one of the important functions of the program is to foster cooperation between scientists working in academia, government, and private industry. Too often, the political considerations and controversiality of the ecological issues created an undesirable barrier between the different groups of scientists. I sincerely hope that the activities of this program will work towards the destruction of these barriers.

Robert Lewis (University of Saarland, Saarbrucken, West Germany).

Following is the scientific and world climate in which the proposed International Cooperative Program in Statistical Ecology for Resource Productivity and Environmental Protection may develop:

1. Numerous regional, national, and global environmental and resource problems are widely recognized.

2. There have been numerous failures of prediction—sometimes because of inadequate data; sometimes because of poor or inappropriate analysis and interpretation.

3. Public bodies and scientists are becoming more sophisticated in dealing with many of these problems. Nevertheless, much subjectivity remains.

4. Both the complexity of identified problems and of the problems that we can deal with has increased. More sophistication and innovation is needed (and this is recognized by many administrators, public policy makers, and involved scientists).

5. More interdisciplinary research, including the collaboration of basic and applied ecologists is essential.

6. The fiscal base of support to science has dwindled over the past decade. Nevertheless, the force of collective scientific opinion still carries substantial weight with the public and with state and federal governments. Resources (dollars and manpower) are thus available to be applied to problems that are identified as important by the scientific community.

7. In the decade of the 1980s, I believe that a more holistic outlook by scientists and the public is developing. We (ecologists) are finally learning how to evaluate problems and to manage environmental resources through systems approaches.

To be viable, in my view, the program must identify and pursue quantitative issues that are either of scientific or social importance or both. Nevertheless, the program must be structured to invite a broad base of participation.

One (or more) institutes should be established—to produce the newsletter, to assure continuity, and coordination. Otherwise, the program can develop through decentralized working groups based on specific areas of expertise and interest—or on a project basis.

I strongly believe that a viable program will require very early in its development a process whereby we learn what the real (or perceived) needs for such a program are in the eyes of ecologists and other "stakeholders." The results of such a stakeholders analysis can then help to develop a framework for the program that will assure commitment by the scientific community and by potential patrons.

Ella Filippone (Passaic River Coalition, Basking Ridge, N.J.).

When a question arises as to whether an institution should be established, the key question becomes "Is there a need?" How would combining ecology and statistics benefit society. The marriage of the two requires an extensive knowledge of both with an ability to cross over and join together principles which have formerly been foreign to each other.

Ecological principles are based on the natural order, while statistics follow a rigid process utilizing a system of numbers and procedures used to prove absolute fact. However, the use of statistics can reinforce ecological premises so that unknowns become closer to absolute.

As an administrator of an environmental institution, I have often sought such verification or justification of ecological idioms. Public administration, my area of expertise, is: (1) the organization and management of people and materials to achieve the purpose of government; and (2) the art and science of management as applied to affairs of state. In fact, public administration may be termed as an integration of the rigid standards and factors associated with the natural and physical sciences with fluid creative qualities, such as judgment and leadership. Dwight Waldo has emphasized that the term "public administration" has two distinct usages: it is an area of intellectual inquiry, a discipline or study, and is a process or activity (Waldo[1]). Quite often the study becomes engaged in the actual implementation of an activity.

Because an administrator must often investigate ways to conduct a research study, select the process deemed most efficient and thorough, and institute plans for undertaking the project interlaced with evaluation checks in order to assure the completion of the project or goal first established, the availability of clearly presented, accurate statistics can be a distinct asset.

Administrators are logically the primary motivators in the establishment of policy. Rational decision-making includes the following steps and should be

[1]D. Waldo, "What is Public Administration?" from *The Study of Public Administration*, Random House, New York; 1955 and as presented in *Classics of Public Administration*, J. M. Shafritz and A. C. Hyde, Eds.

referred to when establishing an International Program for Ecological and Environmental Statistics:

1. Clearly identify the need for such a program.
2. Clarify and rank the goals.
3. List all relevant options or processes for meeting each goal and all available information on them.
4. Predict the consequence of each approach and assess them according to standards, such as efficiency and equity.
5. Select the procedure which comes closest to achieving the goal and is most consistent with the standards of evaluation.

Although the proposed budget for the program suggested by Professor Patil is conservative, many options have been presented which merit careful consideration. This evaluation should be undertaken by a dedicated and knowledgable Board of Trustees, who could be assembled at an international conference so as to achieve economies in organization and deliberation. The membership should be diverse in nationality, background, profession, and experience. All sectors of the economy should be included: business, government, academia, and others concerned with ecological statistics. The governing board should not be composed only of statisticians, but be representative of the multidisciplinary nature of the subject being created.

Since there is limited time, money, and personnel to handle the establishment of a new program, the purpose for its existence must compete for a position on the agenda of financing organizations. When an issue gains prominence, it moves others into less desirable positions; thus, it is necessary for some dedicated persons to demonstrate the value of an International Program of Ecological and Environmental Statistics, so that the case studies or examples may be presented to funding agencies to establish the program.

James Russell Lowell wrote "New occasions teach new duties. Time makes ancient good uncouth" (Clarke[2]). The Institute could build a new approach to dealing with a shift of attitudes which has occurred during the past decade. "Hidden" costs which have arisen in the form of polluted air and water, diminishing resources, urban blight and congestion, and an aesthetically deteriorating landscape require a comprehensive integration of factors capable of being analyzed, hopefully to establish reasons for new values consistent with the social well being of mankind.

Decision makers need to translate information into action, and they must depend on researchers to gather and to summarize the data necessary to shape policy. Questions must be answered, such as: What methods are feasible in the available time? Do the data fit the policy problems? Can they provide adequate conclusions? Do the data involve important biases? What challenges to

---

[2]*Environmental Spectrim*, R. O. Clarke and P. C. List, Eds., VanNostrand, New York, 1974.

their validity are likely to arise? Does the report give all the key details? (Hoaglin[3]).

The establishment of an integrated ecological/statistical program will require much time, dedication, and funding. Since time is uncompromising, the program should go forward, and we should begin today.

Steven Gertz (Roy F. Weston, Inc., Philadelphia, Pa.).

The development of an International Cooperative Program in Statistical Ecology and Environmental Statistics (ICPSEES) is a most formidable task. If the program is to succeed in an efficient manner, careful attention must be paid to its scope, function, structure, membership, and funding. These parameters need early definition and substance, and from them we must develop a flexible, yet well structured long range plan. If this is not done the foundation will be incomplete, and the program may stutter and stumble, and may never come to complete fruition. Following, by category, are my thoughts on this program.

Scope—What are the important ecological and environmental problems now facing man, and what problems are now developing that may impinge on his future welfare and quality of life? And, if we can answer these questions then we must determine those problems and questions that statistics can help answer. Thus, as we do not yet know the questions our scope must be broad and somewhat encompassing. I therefore propose the following scope.

> The International Cooperative Program in Statistical Ecology and Environmental Statistics is a worldwide group of scientists dedicated to the discovery and application of statistical and mathematical techniques for the improvement of man and his environment.
> The group is authorized to perform all legal things in pursuit of its goals that may properly be done by a scientific group.

Function—In pursuit of its goals and in implementing its scope there are many functions that can be fulfilled. At this time it is not possible to identify all those functions nor to comment on their ultimate goodness. However, as a starting point, I recommend evaluating the following functions as to their need, likelihood of obtaining funding, and interests of the group. The functions are: preparation of monographs; preparation of expert committee reports; issuance of a journal; issuance of a newsletter; holding symposia; graduate and postgraduate research fellowships; think tank assessments for government—industry; legal aspects—generic basis; and industrial consulting—problem basis.

Structure—This may well be the critical issue; for as the group is structured so shall it function. Therefore we should use the time tested approach of a strong central management group and a series of strong decentralized technical groups. This allows each technical group to work independently on techni-

---

[3]D. C. Hoaglin, R. J. Light, B. McPeek, F. Mosteller, M. A. Stoto, *Data for Decisions*, Abt Books, Cambridge, Mass., 1982.

cal issues and permits the centralized management group to monitor and manage effectively. The specific function and a brief description of each group and the Board of Directors follows:

> *Board of Directors*—This group shall consist of no more than 12 voting members with the members chosen based on their expertise and affiliations. In order to balance this group representatives shall be chosen worldwide with expertise in such areas as: statistics, ecology, environmental science/engineering, epidemiology, etc.
>
> The responsibilities of this Board are: to set policy; obtain funding; and long-range planning.
>
> *Central Management Group*—This group shall serve as the administrative managers. Their office shall be separate from any of the technical centers. It is this group's responsibility: to implement the Board of Director's policies; implement funding appropriately; and perform all administrative and production functions.
>
> *Technical Groups*—Each of these groups shall be a center of excellence in one or more areas. They define the problems, research the problems, and provide the answers. As such they may produce monographs, reports, articles, etc. Each technical group shall set up its own internal management structure; but shall have one individual and an alternate responsive to the Central Management Group.

Membership—Membership is open to universities, research centers, government agencies, and other not for profit institutions at the BODs discretion.

Funding—Funding can come from a variety of sources such as foundations, governments, industry groups, industrial companies, or various institutes. Until the direction, structure, and function of the group are known, funding sources are conjectural.

Can we set up a viable International Cooperative Program? We can only know if we try.

Bibliography

Fluid Mechanics in Energy Conversion, J. D. Buckmaster, Ed. Society for Industrial and Applied Mathematics, Philadelphia, Pa., 1980.

Environmental Biomonitoring, Assessment, Prediction, and Management—Certain Cases Studies and Related Quantitative Issues, J. Cairns, Jr., G. P. Patil, and W. E. Waters, Eds. International Co-operative Publishing House, Fairland, Md., 1979.

Cantlon, J., "A National Assessment of Research Trends and Needs," A Report on Productivity of Resources and Environments, Institute of Ecology and Holcomb Research Institute.

Quantitative Population Dynamics, D. G. Chapman and V. F. Gallucci, Eds. International Co-operative Publishing House, Fairland, Md., 1981.

Spatial and Temporal Analysis in Ecology, R. M. Cormack and J. K. Ord, Eds. International Co-operative Publishing House, Fairland, Md., 1979.

Sampling Biological Populations, R. M. Cormack, G. P. Patil, and D. S. Robson, Eds. International Co-operative Publishing House, Fairland, Md., 1979.

Ecological Diversity in Theory and Practice, J. F. Grassle, G. P. Patil, W. K. Smith, and C. Taillie, Eds. International Co-operative Publishing House, Fairland, Md., 1979.

Hennemuth, R. C., "Statistical Ecology Initiatives—The General Issue," personal communication.

Hennemuth, R. C. and Patil, G. P., "Implementing Statistical Ecology Initiatives for Global Resource Impacts—An Introduction to the Concept and a Workplan," *Proceedings of a Conference on Renewable Resource Inventories for Monitoring Changes and Trends*, John Bell and Toby Atterbury, Eds., Oregon State University, Corvallis, Oreg., 1983, pp. 374-378.

Hunter, J. S., "Environmental Monitoring, a report to the EPA from the Study Group on Environmental Monitoring, National Academy of Sciences, Washington, D.C., 1977.

Systems Analysis of Ecosystems, G. S. Innis and R. V. O'Neill, Eds. International Co-operative Publishing House, Fairland, Md., 1979.

Epidemiology, D. Ludwig and K. L. Cooke, Eds. Society for Industrial and Applied Mathematics, Philadelphia, Pa., 1975.

Compartmental Analysis of Ecosystem Models, J. H. Matis, B. C. Patten, and G. C. White, Eds. International Co-operative Publishing House, Fairland, Md., 1979.

Statistical Distributions in Ecological Work, J. K. Ord, G. P. Patil, and C. Taillie, Eds. International Co-operative Publishing House, Fairland, Md., 1979.

Multivariate Methods in Ecological Work, L. Orloci, C. R. Rao, and W. M. Stiteler, Eds.. International Co-operative Publishing House, Fairland, Md., 1979.

Patil, G. P., "Satellite Program in Statistical Ecology," *International Statistical Review*, Vol. 47, 1979, pp. 223-228.

Patil, G. P., "Some Perspectives in Statistical Ecology," in *Ecologia*, A. Moroni, O. Ravera, and A. Anelli, Eds., SITE, Parma, Italy, 1981, pp. 181-187.

Patil, G. P., "International Statistical Ecology Program," in *Encyclopedia of Statistical Sciences*, S. Kotz and N. L. Johnson, Eds., Wiley, New York, to appear.

Patil, G. P., "Studies in Statistical Ecology Involving Weighted Distributions," *Proceedings*. ISI Golden Jubilee, Calcutta, India, to appear.

Patil, G. P., "Some Perspectives of Statistical Ecology and the Environmental Statistics," based on keynote speech given at the inaugural of this symposium.

Sampling and Modeling Biological Populations and Population Dynamics, G. P. Patil, E. C. Pielou, and W. E. Waters, Eds. Pennsylvania State University, University Park, Pa., 1971.

Many Species Populations, Ecosystems, and Systems Analysis, G. P. Patil, E. C. Pielou, and W. E. Waters, Eds. Pennsylvania State University Press, University Park, Pa., 1971.

Contemporary Quantitative Ecology and Related Ecometrics, G. P. Patil and M. L. Rosenzweig, Eds. International Co-operative Publishing House, Fairland, Md., 1979.

Energy: Mathematics and Models, F. S. Roberts, Ed. Society for Industrial and Applied Mathematics, Philadelphia, Pa., 1976.

Time Series and Ecological Processes, H. H. Shugart, Ed. Society for Industrial and Applied Mathematics, Philadelphia, Pa., 1978.

Environmetrics 81: Selected Papers, selected papers from a Conference held in Alexandria, Virginia, 8-10 April 1981, Society for Industrial and Applied Mathematics, Philadelphia, Pa.

Skellam, J. G., "Some Philosophical Aspects of Mathematical Modeling in Empirical Science with Special Reference to Ecology, in *Mathematical Models in Ecology*, J. N. R. Jeffers, Ed., Blackwell Scientific Publications, Oxford, 1972, pp. 13-28.

American Statistician, M. Straf, Ed. "Proceedings of the Sixth Symposium on Statistics and the Environment, Vol. 36., 1982.

Train, R. E., "Management for the Future," presented at the National Conference on Managing the Environment, United States Environmental Protection Agency, Washington, D.C., 1973.

Environmental Health Perspectives, DHEW Publication No. (NIH) 72-218, United States Department of Health, Education, and Welfare, Washington, D.C., 1979.

"Third Symposium-Statistics and the Environment, *Journal of the Washington Academy of Sciences*, Vol. 64, No. 2, 1974.

Environmental Health: Quantitative Methods, A. S. Whittemore, Ed. Society for Industrial and Applied Mathematics, Philadelphia, Pa., 1977.

Energy and Health, A. S. Whittemore and N. E. Breslow, Eds. Society for Industrial and Applied Mathematics, Philadelphia, Pa., 1979.

Summary

The papers presented in this volume cover a wide scope in the development and use of mathematics and statistics in the environmental sciences. The areas covered included such diverse topics as biological community structure, risk assessment for environmental health based regulations, and laboratory quality assurance programs. Yet, though all of these diverse areas there has been one central theme, and that was to show the breadth of mathematical and statistical techniques that can be used in environmental studies.

An introductory paper by Patil introduces the topics of statistical ecology and environmental statistics. This paper sets the scene with perspectives on the usefulness of statistics in environmental studies. Examples are given for observational studies such as size based sampling and weighted distributions, aerial surveys and visibility bias, and resource utilization surveys. Extrapolation issues are then discussed and examples of the problems encountered are reviewed. Risk assessment is briefly described. The author notes the variability of the environment and how this variability need be considered in interpreting data and drawing conclusions. Specifically he states that one can only model or interpret the implicit data and develop a correct mathematical statement which may or may not be the scientifically correct statement.

A paper by Smith discusses the design of efficient environmental surveys over time. He states that classical survey methods deal with observations taken at a single point in time and are not applicable to measurements made over time. This is due to correlations between the on-going environmental process and space and time. He presents a worked example to show how an efficient survey through time can be designed. His approach is to divide the subject time interval into a subset of equal time intervals and sample at the midpoint of each discrete subset interval. Equations are then given to optimize the sampling process with respect to cost and allowable variance.

The paper by Hendrickson and Horowitz continued on this theme by examining the statistical analysis of biological community data. They evaluated seven distinct cases where statistical analyses would be appropriate. These cases considered:

1. Analysis of variance and regression on a single species,
2. Gradient analysis on a single variable,
3. Canonical analysis with many environmental variables,
4. A priori contrasts among samples,
5. Species co-variance analysis,
6. Grouping of samples, and
7. Clustering analysis.

Then based on those case studies, they conclude that correctly gathered data can be extensively analyzed to give meaningful results.

Ginzburg et al show the development of a method to evaluate the risk of a population decreasing to some preassigned critical level in a given period of time. They used the Hudson river striped bass to show the effectiveness and limitations of their method. Their method is based on a stochastic age-structured model of population dynamics. A two step process is recommended. The first step constructs the one-dimensional model with the autocorrelated noise term reflecting the underlying multidimensional process. The second step solves the first time passage problem in that one dimension.

Roth et al look at risk assessment in developing health based regulations. They give an overview of strategies being employed to develop health based regulations for air and water quality. It is shown that previous regulations were designed for a zero risk; but obviously this is not possible, and a new strategy is needed. This new strategy is based on assessing the risks associated with various levels of pollution and setting standards at levels which provide reasonable protection. They state that this technique is more defensible from a scientific and cost-benefit standpoint.

Taylor then looks at the essential features of a laboratory quality assurance program. He states that progress in the environmental sciences is highly dependent on reliable data from complex measurement processes. Then, because of this complexity, the measurement process must be well designed and operate in a state of statistical control. The basic elements which he states foster this design and control include: good laboratory practices, standard operational procedures, protocols for specific purposes, and education and training.

The paper by Hensler on statistical and ecological software introduces the readily available programs along with information on obtaining them. He reviews four general statistical systems: P-STAT, SAS, BMDP, and SPSS as well as programs to analyze line transect data, capture-mark-recapture data, capture data, and several others. In his review of these programs he concentrates on their capabilities, portability, ease of learning and usage, and reliability. He does not make any specific recommendations but does provide sufficient information for a potential user to make an informed choice.

The final paper in this volume by Patil reports on the panel discussion concerning a proposed cooperative program on statistical ecology and environmental statistics. This program and the ensuing discussion considered the formulation of prototype and experimental programs such as, cooperative research centers to work on issues involving both scientific and public policy research, timely symposia and workshops, and satellite courses. The eight panelists expressed their positive views on this need and the means whereby it may be fulfilled.

This volume presented an overview on the use of statistical and mathematical techniques in the environmental sciences. There were papers dealing with general conceptual views and there were papers dealing with highly mathematical approaches to specific problems. It is hoped that this volume has shed some light on the use of statistics in the environmental sciences, that ASTM Subcommittee D19.01 will continue its work in this area, and that further progress can be reported in future publications of this sort.

Steven M. Gertz

Roy F. Weston, Inc. West Chester, Pa. 19380.

Index